MW01596050

FLORENCE
RESTAURANT GUIDE

RESTAURANTS, BARS AND CAFES
Your Guide to Authentic Regional Eats

FLORENCE RESTAURANT GUIDE 2022
Best Rated Restaurants in Florence, Italy

© Charles N. Connolly
© E.G.P. Editorial

Printed in USA.

ISBN-13: 9798501036406

Copyright ©
All rights reserved.

FLORENCE RESTAURANT GUIDE

The Most Recommended Restaurants in the City

This directory is dedicated to the Business Owners and Managers who provide the experience that the locals and tourists enjoy. Thanks you very much for all that you do and thank for being the "People Choice".

Thanks to everyone that posts their reviews online and the amazing reviews sites that make our life easier.

The places listed in this book are the most positively reviewed and recommended by locals and travelers from around the world.

Thank you for your time and enjoy the directory that is designed with locals and tourist in mind!

TOP 500
RESTAURANTS
Ranked from #1 to #500

#1
Pensavo Peggio
Cuisines: Italian
Average Price: Modest
Area: Santa Maria
Address: Via Del Moro 51R 50123
Florence Italy
Phone: 055 2302987

#2
Trattoria Zà Zà
Cuisines: Italian
Average Price: Modest
Area: Santa Maria
Address: Piazza Del Mercato Centrale 26R
50123 Florence Italy
Phone: 055 215411

#3
Trattoria Da Mario
Cuisines: Tuscan
Average Price: Modest
Area: Santa Maria
Address: Via Rosina 2R 50100
Florence Italy
Phone: 055 218550

#4
La Giostra
Cuisines: Tuscan
Average Price: Expensive
Area: Duomo
Address: Borgo Pinti 10R 50121
Florence Italy
Phone: 055 241341

#5
Mercato Centrale Firenze
Cuisines: Italian, Cafes, Steakhouses
Average Price: Modest
Area: Santa Maria
Address: Piazza Del Mercato Centrale 4
50100 Florence Italy
Phone: 055 2399798

#6
Trattoria Dall'oste
Cuisines: Italian, Trattorie, Steakhouses
Average Price: Expensive
Area: Duomo
Address: Via Dei Cerchi 40R 50122
Florence Italy
Phone: 055 213142

#7
Trattoria Giovanni
Cuisines: Tuscan
Average Price: Modest
Area: Palazzo Pitti
Address: Via Sant'Agostino 38R 50125
Florence Italy
Phone: 371 1940715

#8
All'Antico Vinaio
Cuisines: Sandwiches
Average Price: Inexpensive
Area: Duomo
Address: Via Dei Neri 74R 50122
Florence Italy
Phone: 055 2382723

#9
Trattoria Pallottino
Cuisines: Tuscan
Average Price: Modest
Area: Duomo
Address: Via Isola Delle Stinche 1R 50122
Florence Italy
Phone: 055 2608887

#10
Gusta Pizza
Cuisines: Italian, Pizza
Average Price: Inexpensive
Area: Palazzo Pitti
Address: Via Maggio 46R 50125
Florence Italy
Phone: 055 285068

#11
Osteria Del Cinghiale Bianco
Cuisines: Tuscan
Average Price: Expensive
Area: Palazzo Pitti
Address: Borgo San Iacopo 43R 50125
Florence Italy
Phone: 055 215706

#12
Vini E Vecchi Sapori
Cuisines: Tuscan
Average Price: Modest
Area: Duomo
Address: Via Dei Magazzini 3R 50122
Florence Italy
Phone: 055 293045

#13
Osteria Di Poneta
Cuisines: Steakhouses, Italian
Average Price: Modest
Area: Novoli
Address: Via Di Novoli 73C 50127
Florence Italy
Phone: 055 411082

#14
Trattoria Da Tito
Cuisines: Italian, Steakhouses
Average Price: Modest
Area: Indipendenza
Address: Via San Gallo 112R 50129
Florence Italy
Phone: 055 472475

#15
Trattoria Da Giorgio
Cuisines: Tuscan, Abruzzese
Average Price: Modest
Area: Santa Maria
Address: Via Del Palazzuolo 100R 50123
Florence Italy
Phone: 055 284302

#16
Taverna Del Bronzino
Cuisines: Tuscan
Average Price: Modest
Area: Indipendenza
Address: Via Delle Ruote 27R 50129
Florence Italy
Phone: 055 495220

#17
Osteria Santo Spirito
Cuisines: Tuscan
Average Price: Modest
Area: Palazzo Pitti
Address: Piazza Santo Spirito 16R 50125
Florence Italy
Phone: 055 2382383

#18
La Bussola
Cuisines: Italian, Pizza, Wine Bars
Average Price: Modest
Area: Duomo
Address: Via Porta Rossa 58R 50123
Florence Italy
Phone: 055 293376

#19
Il Pizzaiuolo
Cuisines: Pizza, Italian
Average Price: Modest
Area: Santa Croce
Address: Via Dei Macci 113 50122
Florence Italy
Phone: 055 241171

#20
La Continetta
Cuisines: Italian, Wine Bars
Average Price: Modest
Area: Duomo
Address: Borgo San Lorenzo 14R 50123
Florence Italy
Phone: 055 213525

#21
Osteria Vecchio Vicolo
Cuisines: Italian
Average Price: Modest
Area: Duomo
Address: Via Lambertesca 16R 50122
Florence Italy
Phone: 055 2654512

#22
La Prosciutteria
Cuisines: Tuscan, Wine Bars
Average Price: Modest
Area: Duomo
Address: Via Dei Neri 54R 50122
Florence Italy
Phone: 055 2654472

#23
Trattoria Nella
Cuisines: Italian, Jazz & Blues
Average Price: Modest
Area: Duomo
Address: Via Delle Terme 19R 50123
Florence Italy
Phone: 055 218925

#24
L'osteria Di Giovanni
Cuisines: Tuscan
Average Price: Expensive
Area: Santa Maria
Address: Via Del Moro 22 50123
Florence Italy
Phone: 055 284897

#25
Trattoria Guelfa
Cuisines: Italian, Trattorie
Average Price: Modest
Area: Indipendenza
Address: Via Guelfa 103 50129
Florence Italy
Phone: 055 213306

#26
Trattoria Sostanza
Cuisines: Trattorie, Italian
Average Price: Expensive
Area: Santa Maria
Address: Via Del Porcellana 25R 50123
Florence Italy
Phone: 055 212691

#27
Paperorosso
Cuisines: Italian
Average Price: Modest
Area: Stazione Ferroviaria Santa Maria
Address: Via Montebello 86 50123
Florence Italy
Phone: 055 218891

#28
Trattoria Boboli
Cuisines: Wine Bars, Tuscan
Average Price: Modest
Area: Palazzo Pitti
Address: Via Romana 45R 50125
Florence Italy
Phone: 055 2336401

#29
Ciri Bé
Cuisines: Italian, Pizza
Average Price: Modest
Area: Novoli
Address: Via Antonio Pigafetta 10 50127
Florence Italy
Phone: 055 432623

#30
Trattoria Pizzeria Santa Lucia
Cuisines: Pizza
Average Price: Modest
Area: Le Cascine
Address: Via Del Ponte Alle Mosse 102R
50144
Florence Italy
Phone: 055 353255

#31
Trattoria La Casalinga
Cuisines: Tuscan
Average Price: Modest
Area: Palazzo Pitti
Address: Via Dei Michelozzi 9R 50125
Florence Italy
Phone: 055 218624

#33
l' Brindellone
Cuisines: Tuscan
Average Price: Modest
Area: Palazzo Pitti
Address: Piazza Piattellina 10 50124
Florence Italy
Phone: 055 217879

#32
La Boite
Cuisines: Italian, Wine Bars, Cocktail Bars
Average Price: Inexpensive
Area: Santa Maria
Address: Piazza San Paolino 3R 50123
Florence Italy
Phone: 055 213928

#34
Trattoria Cesarino
Cuisines: Trattorie
Average Price: Modest
Area: Santa Croce
Address: Via Niccolini Giovan Battista 16R
50121 Florence Italy
Phone: 055 2479169

#35
Ristorante Natalino
Cuisines: Beer, Wine & Spirits, Tuscan
Average Price: Modest
Area: Duomo
Address: Borgo Albizi 17R 50122
Florence Italy
Phone: 055 289404

#36
Fuoco Matto
Cuisines: Pizza
Average Price: Modest
Area: Indipendenza
Address: Via Ventisette Aprile 16 50129
Florence Italy
Phone: 055 495140

#37
Trattoria La Burrasca
Cuisines: Italian, Trattorie
Average Price: Modest
Area: Santa Maria
Address: Via Panicale 6R 50123
Florence Italy
Phone: 055 215827

#38
La Beppa Fioraia
Cuisines: Tuscan, Pizza
Average Price: Modest
Area: Michelangelo
Address: Via Erta Canina 6R 50125
Florence Italy
Phone: 055 2347681

#39
Osteria Pastella
Cuisines: Tuscan, Mediterranean
Average Price: Expensive
Area: Santa Maria
Address: Via Della Scala 17R 50123
Florence Italy
Phone: 055 2670240

#40
Osteria Pepò
Cuisines: Tuscan
Average Price: Modest
Area: Santa Maria
Address: Via Rosina 4R 50123
Florence Italy
Phone: 055 283259

#41
I Bastioni Di San Niccolò
Cuisines: Pizza, Sandwiches, Italian
Average Price: Modest
Area: Michelangelo
Address: Via Dei Bastioni 9R 50125
Florence Italy
Phone: 055 2476760

#42
Osteria I Riffaioli
Cuisines: Italian
Average Price: Modest
Area: Piazza Della Liberta/Savonarola
Address: Via Ponte Alle Riffe 2 50133
Florence Italy
Phone: 055 5088070

#43
Trattoria Il Giova
Cuisines: Italian
Average Price: Modest
Area: Santa Croce
Address: Borgo La Croce 73R 50121
Florence Italy
Phone: 055 2480639

#44
Trattoria Marione
Cuisines: Tuscan
Average Price: Modest
Area: Santa Maria
Address: Via Della Spada 27R 50123
Florence Italy
Phone: 055 214756

#45
Trattoria Gigi
Cuisines: Italian
Average Price: Modest
Area: Michelangelo
Address: Via Giampaolo Orsini 32R 50126
Florence Italy
Phone: 055 6810474

#46
Il Santo Bevitore
Cuisines: Italian
Average Price: Expensive
Area: Palazzo Pitti
Address: Via Santo Spirito 64R 50125
Florence Italy
Phone: 055 211264

#47
Borderline
Cuisines: Seafood, Tuscan
Average Price: Expensive
Area: Stazione Ferroviaria Santa Maria
Address: Corso Italia 35 50123
Florence Italy
Phone: 055 288771

#48
Trattoria Da Benvenuto
Cuisines: Tuscan, Trattorie
Average Price: Modest
Area: Duomo
Address: Via Della Mosca 16R 50122
Florence Italy
Phone: 055 214833

#49
Trattoria 4 Leoni
Cuisines: Italian
Average Price: Expensive
Area: Palazzo Pitti
Address: Via De' Vellutini 1R 50125
Florence Italy
Phone: 055 218562

#50
Da Nasone
Cuisines: Pizza, Italian
Average Price: Modest
Area: Indipendenza
Address: Via Santa Caterina D'alessandria
3R 50129 Florence Italy
Phone: 324 0950326

#51
Il Santino
Cuisines: Beer, Wine & Spirits, Tuscan
Average Price: Modest
Area: Palazzo Pitti
Address: Via Di Santo Spirito 60R 50125
Florence Italy
Phone: 055 2302820

#52
Buca Mario
Cuisines: Tuscan
Average Price: Exclusive
Area: Santa Maria
Address: Piazza Degli Ottaviani 16R 50123
Florence Italy
Phone: 055 214179

#53
Boutique Della Pasta Fresca
Cuisines: Pasta Shops, Tuscan
Average Price: Inexpensive
Area: Piazza Della Liberta/Savonarola
Address: Via Domenico Cirillo 2C 50133
Florence Italy
Phone: 055 578087

#54
Il Barretto
Cuisines: Tuscan, Seafood
Average Price: Modest
Area: Santa Maria
Address: Via Del Parione 50R 50123
Florence Italy
Phone: 055 294122

#55
Zeb
Cuisines: Tuscan, Soup
Average Price: Expensive
Area: Michelangelo
Address: Via San Miniato 2R 50125
Florence Italy
Phone: 055 2342864

#56
Mangia Pizza
Cuisines: Pizza
Average Price: Inexpensive
Area: Duomo
Address: Via Lambertesca 24R 50122
Florence Italy
Phone: 055 287595

#57
Hosteria Del Bricco
Cuisines: Tuscan
Average Price: Expensive
Area: Michelangelo
Address: Via San Niccolo 8R 50125
Florence Italy
Phone: 055 2345037

#58
Pizzeria San Jacopino
Cuisines: Pizza, Tuscan
Average Price: Modest
Area: Le Cascine
Address: Piazza San Jacopino 30R 50144
Florence Italy
Phone: 055 333195

#59
Lo Sprone Vinaino
Cuisines: Italian
Average Price: Inexpensive
Area: Palazzo Pitti
Address: Via Dello Sprone 17R 50125
Florence Italy
Phone: 055 219508

#60
Trattoria 13 Gobbi
Cuisines: Tuscan, Steakhouses
Average Price: Expensive
Area: Santa Maria
Address: Via Del Porcellana 9R 50123
Florence Italy
Phone: 055 284015

#61
Osteria Antica Mescita San Niccolò
Cuisines: Tuscan
Average Price: Modest
Area: Michelangelo
Address: Via San Niccolò 60R 50126
Florence Italy
Phone: 055 2342836

#62
La Loggia
Cuisines: Italian
Average Price: Expensive
Area: Michelangelo
Address: Piazzale Michelangelo 1 50125
Florence Italy
Phone: 055 2342832

#63
Culinaria Bistro De Gustibus
Cuisines: Wine Bars, Bistros, Mediterranean
Average Price: Modest
Area: Palazzo Pitti
Address: Piazza Torquato Tasso 13R 50124
Florence Italy
Phone: 055 229494

#64
Benedicta
Cuisines: Italian
Average Price: Modest
Area: Santa Maria
Address: Via Benedetta 12R 50123
Florence Italy
Phone: 055 2645429

#65
Alfredo
Cuisines: Italian, Pizza
Average Price: Modest
Area: Piazza Della Liberta/Savonarola
Address: Viale Don Giovanni Minzoni 3
50133 Florence Italy
Phone: 055 578291

#66
Ostaria Dei Centopoveri
Cuisines: Pizza, Italian
Average Price: Modest
Area: Santa Maria
Address: Via Palazzuolo 31R 50123
Florence Italy
Phone: 055 218846

#67
Finisterrae
Cuisines: Italian, Mediterranean, Pizza
Average Price: Modest
Area: Santa Croce
Address: Piazza Santa Croce 12 50122
Florence Italy
Phone: 055 2638675

#68
Fratelli Briganti
Cuisines: Tuscan, Pizza
Average Price: Modest
Area: Fortezza Basso
Address: Piazza Giovanbattista Giorgini 12R
50134 Florence Italy
Phone: 055 475255

#69
Trattoria Il Contadino
Cuisines: Italian
Average Price: Modest
Area: Santa Maria
Address: Via Palazzuolo 71R 50123
Florence Italy
Phone: 055 2382673

#70
Trattoria Acquacotta
Cuisines: Italian
Average Price: Expensive
Area: Santa Croce
Address: Via De Pilastri 51R 50121
Florence Italy
Phone: 055 242907

#71
Osteria Il Gatto E La Volpe
Cuisines: Pizza, Italian
Average Price: Modest
Area: Duomo
Address: Via Ghibellina 151R 50122
Florence Italy
Phone: 055 289264

#72
Giglio Rosso
Cuisines: Italian
Average Price: Modest
Area: Santa Maria
Address: Via Panzani 35R 50123
Florence Italy
Phone: 055 211795

#73
Osteria Ganino
Cuisines: Tuscan
Average Price: Modest
Area: Duomo
Address: Piazza Dei Cimatori 4R 50122
Florence Italy
Phone: 055 214125

#74
Trattoria Antellesi
Cuisines: Italian
Average Price: Modest
Area: Santa Maria
Address: Via Faenza 9R 50123
Florence Italy
Phone: 055 216990

#75
Il Profeta
Cuisines: Tuscan
Average Price: Expensive
Area: Stazione Ferroviaria Santa Maria
Address: Borgo Ognissanti I 93R 50123
Florence Italy
Phone: 055 212265

#76
Le Volpi E l'Uva
Cuisines: Beer, Wine & Spirits, Tuscan
Average Price: Modest
Area: Palazzo Pitti
Address: Piazza Dei Rossi 1R 50125
Florence Italy
Phone: 055 2398132

#77
Osteria Dell'olio
Cuisines: Italian, Mediterranean
Average Price: Expensive
Area: Duomo
Address: Piazza Dell'olio 10R 50123
Florence Italy
Phone: 055 211466

#78
Ristorante Accademia
Cuisines: Tuscan
Average Price: Expensive
Area: Duomo
Address: Piazza San Marco 7R 50121
Florence Italy
Phone: 055 217343

#79
Da Nerbone
Cuisines: Tuscan, Sandwiches
Average Price: Inexpensive
Area: Santa Maria
Address: Piazza Mercato Centrale 47R
50123 Florence Italy
Phone: 055 219949

#80
Perseus
Cuisines: Steakhouses
Average Price: Expensive
Area: Piazza Della Liberta/Savonarola
Address: Viale Don Giovanni Minzoni 10R
50129 Florence Italy
Phone: 055 588226

#81
Al Tranvai
Cuisines: Tuscan, Trattorie
Average Price: Modest
Area: Palazzo Pitti
Address: Piazza Tasso Torquato 14R 50124
Florence Italy
Phone: 055 225197

#82
La Bocca Di Leone
Cuisines: Italian
Average Price: Modest
Area: Palazzo Pitti
Address: Via Pisana 39R 50100
Florence Italy
Phone: 055 2286572

#83
Alla Vecchia Bettola
Cuisines: Tuscan
Average Price: Expensive
Area: Palazzo Pitti
Address: Viale Vasco Pratolini 3 50124
Florence Italy
Phone: 055 224158

#84
Strapizzami
Cuisines: Pizza, Italian
Average Price: Modest
Area: Campo Di Marte
Address: Via Dei Sette Santi 29R 50131
Florence Italy
Phone: 055 577112

#85
Farina 00
Cuisines: Italian, Pizza, Sandwiches
Average Price: Modest
Area: Indipendenza
Address: Viale Giacomo Matteotti 30 50132
Florence Italy
Phone: 055 4089038

#86
Il Portale
Cuisines: Pizza, Italian
Average Price: Expensive
Area: Stazione Ferroviaria Santa Maria
Address: Via Luigi Alamanni 29R 50123
Florence Italy
Phone: 055 212992

#87
Chicco Di Caffè
Cuisines: Italian
Average Price: Modest
Area: Palazzo Pitti
Address: Via Della Chiesa 16R 50123
Florence Italy
Phone: 055 2654354

#88
Tamerò
Cuisines: Italian
Average Price: Modest
Area: Palazzo Pitti
Address: Piazza Santo Spirito 11 50125
Florence Italy
Phone: 055 282596

#89
Ic Che Thai
Cuisines: Thai
Average Price: Modest
Area: Piazza Della Liberta/Savonarola
Address: Via Pier Capponi 72A 50132
Florence Italy
Phone: 055 3843387

#90
Il Rifrullo
Cuisines: Bars, Tuscan
Average Price: Modest
Area: Michelangelo
Address: Via San Niccolò 53 50125
Florence Italy
Phone: 055 2342621

#91
Trattoria Armando
Cuisines: Tuscan
Average Price: Expensive
Area: Stazione Ferroviaria Santa Maria
Address: Borgo Ognissanti 140R 50123
Florence Italy
Phone: 055 217263

#92
Trattoria Del Pennello
Cuisines: Italian, Trattorie, Seafood
Average Price: Modest
Area: Duomo
Address: Via Alighieri Dante 4R 50122
Florence Italy
Phone: 055 294848

#93
Cipiglio
Cuisines: Pizza
Average Price: Modest
Area: Fortezza Basso
Address: Via Lambruschini Raffaello 15R
50134
Florence Italy
Phone: 055 490804

#94
L'Angolo
Cuisines: Chinese
Average Price: Inexpensive
Area: Santa Maria
Address: Via Dell'ariento 18R 50123
Florence Italy
Phone: 055 2645797

#95
La Grotta Guelfa
Cuisines: Tuscan
Average Price: Modest
Area: Duomo
Address: Via Pellicceria 5R 50123
Florence Italy
Phone: 055 210042

#96
Trattoria San Lorenzo
Cuisines: Italian, Trattorie
Average Price: Modest
Area: Duomo
Address: Via Borgo San Lorenzo 53R 50123
Florence Italy
Phone: 055 2670414

#97
La Grotta
Cuisines: Tuscan
Average Price: Inexpensive
Area: Fortezza Basso
Address: Via Bolognese 14R 50139
Florence Italy
Phone: 055 480405

#98
Don Fefè
Cuisines: Pizza, Seafood, Steakhouses
Average Price: Modest
Area: Piazza Della Liberta/Savonarola
Address: Via Giuseppe La Farina 29 50132
Florence Italy
Phone: 055 576763

#99
Il Latini
Cuisines: Tuscan
Average Price: Expensive
Area: Santa Maria
Address: Via Dei Palchetti 6R 50123
Florence Italy
Phone: 055 210916

#100
Coquinarius
Cuisines: Wine Bars, Italian
Average Price: Modest
Area: Duomo
Address: Via Delle Oche 11R 50122
Florence Italy
Phone: 055 2302153

#101
Baldovino
Cuisines: Italian, Pizza, Bistros
Average Price: Modest
Area: Santa Croce
Address: Via Di San Giuseppe 22R 50122
Florence Italy
Phone: 055 241773

#102
La Ghiotta
Cuisines: Italian
Average Price: Modest
Area: Santa Croce
Address: Via Pietrapiana 7R 50121
Florence Italy
Phone: 055 241237

#103
Cacio Vino Trallallà
Cuisines: Wine Bars, Italian
Average Price: Expensive
Area: Duomo
Address: Borgo Strada Statale Apostoli 29R
50123 Florence Italy
Phone: 055 215558

#104
Trattoria L' Parione
Cuisines: Tuscan
Average Price: Expensive
Area: Santa Maria
Address: Via Del Parione 74R 50123
Florence Italy
Phone: 055 214005

#105
La Pentola Dell'oro
Cuisines: Tuscan
Average Price: Modest
Area: Santa Croce
Address: Via Di Mezzo 24 50121
Florence Italy
Phone: 055 241808

#106
La Fettunta
Cuisines: Tuscan, Burgers, Sandwiches
Average Price: Modest
Area: Duomo
Address: Via Dei Neri 72R 50122
Florence Italy
Phone: 055 2741102

#107
Trattoria Baldini
Cuisines: Italian
Average Price: Expensive
Area: Stazione Ferroviaria Santa Maria
Address: Via Il Prato 96R 50100
Florence Italy
Phone: 055 287663

#108
Del Fagioli
Cuisines: Italian
Average Price: Modest
Area: Santa Croce
Address: Corso Dei Tintori 47R 50122
Florence Italy
Phone: 055 244285

#109
Baraka Cafe'
Cuisines: Lounges, Italian
Average Price: Inexpensive
Area: Novoli
Address: Via Di Novoli 75R 50127
Florence Italy
Phone: 055 431495

#110
Trattoria Dell'orto
Cuisines: Italian
Average Price: Expensive
Area: Palazzo Pitti
Address: Via Dell'orto 35A 50124
Florence Italy
Phone: 055 224148

#111
Luci Al Piazzale
Cuisines: Italian, Cocktail Bars
Average Price: Modest
Area: Michelangelo
Address: Viale Michelangelo 61 50125
Florence Italy
Phone: 338 3519317

#112
Trattoria Gozzi
Cuisines: Tuscan
Average Price: Modest
Area: Santa Maria
Address: Piazza Di San Lorenzo 8R 50123
Florence Italy
Phone: 055 281941

#113
Il Giardino
Cuisines: Italian
Average Price: Modest
Area: Stazione Ferroviaria Santa Maria
Address: Via Della Scala 61 50123
Florence Italy
Phone: 055 213141

#114
7 Rosso
Cuisines: Italian
Average Price: Expensive
Area: Bosco Bello
Address: Via San Domenico 103A 50133
Florence Italy
Phone: 055 580812

#115
La Vinaina
Cuisines: Tuscan
Average Price: Modest
Area: Santa Croce
Address: Via Dell' Agnolo 48R 50122
Florence Italy
Phone: 055 2344120

#116
Pizzeria Spera
Cuisines: Pizza
Average Price: Modest
Area: Fortezza Basso
Address: Via Della Cernaia 9R 50129
Florence Italy
Phone: 055 495286

#117
Boccadama
Cuisines: Italian
Average Price: Modest
Area: Santa Croce
Address: Piazza Di Santa Croce 25R 50122
Florence Italy
Phone: 055 243640

#118
Irene
Cuisines: Italian
Average Price: Expensive
Area: Duomo
Address: Piazza Della Repubblica 7 50123
Florence Italy
Phone: 055 2735891

#119
La Terrazza
Cuisines: Cafes, Italian
Average Price: Modest
Area: Duomo
Address: La Rinascente 50123
Florence Italy
Phone: 055 283612

#120
Trattoria Alfredo
Cuisines: Italian, Trattorie
Average Price: Modest
Area: Duomo
Address: Via Dei Leoni 14 50122
Florence Italy
Phone: 055 294912

#121
Trattoria Bordino
Cuisines: Trattorie
Average Price: Modest
Area: Palazzo Pitti
Address: Via Stracciatella 9R 50125
Florence Italy
Phone: 055 213048

#122
Antica Trattoria Tre Soldi
Cuisines: Tuscan
Average Price: Expensive
Area: Campo Di Marte
Address: Via Gabriele d'Annunzio 4R A
50135 Florence Italy
Phone: 055 679366

#123
Trattoria I' Grullo
Cuisines: Italian, Trattorie
Average Price: Modest
Area: Duomo
Address: Via Dei Servi 51R 50122
Florence Italy
Phone: 055 280802

#124
Mastro Ciliegia
Cuisines: Italian, Pizza
Average Price: Modest
Area: Duomo
Address: Via Matteo Palmieri 12 50122
Florence Italy
Phone: 055 2480964

#125
Osteria Delle Tre Panche
Cuisines: Italian
Average Price: Expensive
Area: Campo Di Marte
Address: Via Pacinotti Antonio 32R 50131
Florence Italy
Phone: 055 583724

#126
Osteria Toscanella
Cuisines: Italian
Average Price: Expensive
Area: Palazzo Pitti
Address: Via Toscanella 36R 50125
Florence Italy
Phone: 055 285488

#127
Caffè Dell'oro
Cuisines: Cocktail Bars, Italian
Average Price: Expensive
Area: Duomo
Address: Lungarno Degli Acciaiuoli 2P 50123
Florence Italy
Phone: 055 27268912

#128
Il Borro Tuscan Bistro
Cuisines: Bistros, Tuscan
Average Price: Expensive
Area: Duomo
Address: Lungarno Acciaiuoli 80R 50123
Florence Italy
Phone: 055 290423

#129
Fratelli Cuore
Cuisines: Pizza, Italian
Average Price: Modest
Area: Santa Maria
Address: Piazza Della Stazione 50123
Florence Italy
Phone: 055 2670264

#130
l'Giuggiolo
Cuisines: Tuscan, Pizza
Average Price: Modest
Area: Campo Di Marte
Address: Viale Righi Augusto 3A 50137
Florence Italy
Phone: 055 606240

#131
Brewdog
Cuisines: Breweries, Pubs, Burgers
Average Price: Inexpensive
Area: Santa Maria
Address: Via Faenza 21R 50123
Florence Italy
Phone: 055 217035

#132
Boccadarno
Cuisines: Seafood, Bistros, Wine Bars
Average Price: Modest
Area: Michelangelo
Address: Via San Niccolo 56R 50125
Florence Italy
Phone: 055 3860860

#133
Sweet
Cuisines: Italian, Wine Bars
Average Price: Modest
Area: Michelangelo
Address: Via Di Ripoli 8 50126
Florence Italy
Phone: 055 6587051

#134
Il Vezzo
Cuisines: Italian, Mediterranean
Average Price: Modest
Area: Indipendenza
Address: Via Guelfa 58R 50123
Florence Italy
Phone: 055 281096

#135
Ristoranti Celestino
Cuisines: Italian
Average Price: Expensive
Area: Palazzo Pitti
Address: Piazza S. Felicita, 4R 50100
Florence Italy
Phone: 055 2396574

#136
Bistrot Outside
Cuisines: Pizza, Italian
Average Price: Expensive
Area: Oberdan
Address: Lungarno Del Tempio 52 50121
Florence Italy
Phone: 055 2343693

#137
Buca Dell'Orafo
Cuisines: Tuscan
Average Price: Expensive
Area: Duomo
Address: Via De' Girolami 28R 50122
Florence Italy
Phone: 055 213619

#138
Cantinetta Allegri
Cuisines: Tuscan, Steakhouses
Average Price: Modest
Area: Santa Croce
Address: Borgo Allegri 58R 50122
Florence Italy
Phone: 055 2478987

#139
Antica Osteria 1 Rosso
Cuisines: Tuscan
Average Price: Exclusive
Area: Santa Maria
Address: Borgo Ognissanti 1R 50123
Florence Italy
Phone: 055 2670461

#140
Il Paiolo
Cuisines: Tuscan, Trattorie, Steakhouses
Average Price: Expensive
Area: Duomo
Address: Via Del Corso 42R 50122
Florence Italy
Phone: 055 215019

#141
Pulcinella Pizzaiolo
Cuisines: Pizza
Average Price: Inexpensive
Area: Novoli
Address: Via Circondaria 38R 50134
Florence Italy
Phone: 055 330330

#142
Sanfrediavino
Cuisines: Tuscan, Beer, Wine & Spirits
Average Price: Expensive
Area: Palazzo Pitti
Address: Via Pisana 10R 50143
Florence Italy
Phone: 055 229111

#143
Bondi Focaccine
Cuisines: Pizza, Sandwiches
Average Price: Inexpensive
Area: Santa Maria
Address: Via Dell'ariento 85R 50123
Florence Italy
Phone: 055 287390

#144
Trattoria Camillo Cavour
Cuisines: Italian
Average Price: Modest
Area: Indipendenza
Address: Via Cavour 41R 50129
Florence Italy
Phone: 055 2670400

#145
Ristorante La Maremma
Cuisines: Tuscan
Average Price: Modest
Area: Santa Croce
Address: Via Verdi Giuseppe 16R 50122
Florence Italy
Phone: 055 244615

#146
Fiaschetteria Di Pesce
Cuisines: Seafood Markets, Seafood
Average Price: Modest
Area: Palazzo Pitti
Address: Piazza Taddeo Gaddi 5R 50142
Florence Italy
Phone: 055 706492

#147
Accà Ristopizzaperitivo
Cuisines: Napoletana, Pizza
Average Price: Modest
Area: Palazzo Pitti
Address: Via Pisana 120R 50145
Florence Italy
Phone: 055 0351005

#148
La Cucina Del Garga
Cuisines: Italian, Cooking Schools, Seafood
Average Price: Expensive
Area: Indipendenza
Address: Via San Zanobi 33R 50129
Florence Italy
Phone: 055 475286

#149
I Tuscani 2
Cuisines: Steakhouses
Average Price: Expensive
Area: Santa Maria
Address: Via De Federighi 37R 50123
Florence Italy
Phone: 055 9065507

#150
Nedo - L'officina Dei Golosi
Cuisines: Italian, Bistros
Average Price: Modest
Area: Monticelli
Address: Piazza Paolo Uccello 12 50142
Florence Italy
Phone: 055 715246

#151
Mostodolce
Cuisines: Breweries, Italian, Pizza
Average Price: Modest
Area: Santa Maria
Address: Via Nazionale 114 50123
Florence Italy
Phone: 055 2302928

#152
Johnny Bruschetta
Cuisines: Tuscan, Gluten-Free, Vegetarian
Average Price: Modest
Area: Santa Croce
Address: Via De Macci 77R 50122
Florence Italy
Phone: 055 2478326

#153
La Cocotte
Cuisines: Cafes, Italian, Burgers
Average Price: Modest
Area: Oberdan
Address: Via Vincenzo Gioberti 91R 50121
Florence Italy
Phone: 055 662529

#154
Cucina 16
Cuisines: Italian
Average Price: Modest
Area: Campo Di Marte
Address: Via Aretina 16R 50136
Florence Italy
Phone: 055 679867

#155
Trattoria I Due G
Cuisines: Tuscan
Average Price: Modest
Area: Santa Maria
Address: Via Cennini Bernardo 6R 50123
Florence Italy
Phone: 055 218623

#156
Benvenuti A Sud
Cuisines: Pizza, Friterie, Panzerotti
Average Price: Inexpensive
Area: Novoli
Address: Viale Guidoni 83A 50127
Florence Italy
Phone: 055 4476461

#157
La Ménagère
Cuisines: Cocktail Bars, Italian, Cafes
Average Price: Modest
Area: Santa Maria
Address: Via Ginori 8R 50123
Florence Italy
Phone: 055 0750600

#158
Il Palagio
Cuisines: Italian
Average Price: Exclusive
Area: Santa Croce, Indipendenza
Address: Borgo Pinti 99 50121
Florence Italy
Phone: 055 2626450

#159
Relais Le Jardin
Cuisines: Italian
Average Price: Expensive
Area: Santa Croce
Address: Piazza Massimo d'Azeglio 3 50121
Florence Italy
Phone: 055 245247

#160
Osteria Il Grappolo
Cuisines: Italian
Average Price: Modest
Area: Campo Di Marte
Address: Viale Eleonora Duse 6 50137
Florence Italy
Phone: 055 602373

#161
Trattoria Anita
Cuisines: Tuscan
Average Price: Modest
Area: Duomo
Address: Via Del Parlascio 2R 50122
Florence Italy
Phone: 055 218698

#162
Vivanda
Cuisines: Italian, Health Markets, Vegetarian
Average Price: Modest
Area: Palazzo Pitti
Address: Via Santa Monaca 7R 50124
Florence Italy
Phone: 055 2381208

#163
Il Coco
Cuisines: Italian, Korean
Average Price: Expensive
Area: Santa Maria
Address: Via Guelfa 24 50129
Florence Italy
Phone: 055 214977

#164
Gangnam
Cuisines: Barbeque, Korean
Average Price: Modest
Area: Santa Maria, Indipendenza
Address: Via Guelfa 94R 50123
Florence Italy
Phone: 055 3842434

#165
Osteria I' Brincello
Cuisines: Tuscan
Average Price: Modest
Area: Santa Maria
Address: Via Nazionale 110 50123
Florence Italy
Phone: 055 282645

#166
Trattoria BBQ
Cuisines: Barbeque, Italian
Average Price: Expensive
Area: Palazzo Pitti
Address: Piazza Torquato Tasso 9R 50124
Florence Italy
Phone: 055 5120376

#167
Il Pasha
Cuisines: Tuscan
Average Price: Exclusive
Area: Michelangelo
Address: Viale Niccolò Macchiavelli 18 50125
Florence Italy
Phone: 055 228790

#168
Trattoria Antico Fattore
Cuisines: Italian
Average Price: Expensive
Area: Duomo
Address: Via Lambertesca 3 50122
Florence Italy
Phone: 055 288975

#169
Impressione Chongqing
Cuisines: Chinese
Average Price: Modest
Area: Santa Maria
Address: Via Sant Antonino 34R 50123
Florence Italy
Phone: 055 290010

#170
La Grotta Di Leo
Cuisines: Pizza
Average Price: Modest
Area: Santa Maria
Address: Via Della Scala 41R 50123
Florence Italy
Phone: 055 219265

#171
Lo Stravizio
Cuisines: Pizza, Tuscan, Seafood
Average Price: Inexpensive
Area: Gavinana
Address: Via Carlo d'Angiò 60 50126
Florence Italy
Phone: 055 6801370

#172
I 2 Fratellini
Cuisines: Sandwiches, Wine Bars, Salumerie
Average Price: Inexpensive
Area: Duomo
Address: Via Dei Cimatori 38R 50122
Florence Italy
Phone: 055 2396096

#173
Panbriaco
Cuisines: Pizza
Average Price: Inexpensive
Area: Santa Maria
Address: Via Faenza 13R 50123
Florence Italy
Phone: 055 9752513

#174
Le Fonticine
Cuisines: Italian
Average Price: Expensive
Area: Santa Maria
Address: Via Nazionale 79 50123
Florence Italy
Phone: 055 282106

#175
Ciro & Sons
Cuisines: Italian, Pizza, Gluten-Free
Average Price: Modest
Area: Santa Maria
Address: Via Del Giglio 28R 50123
Florence Italy
Phone: 055 289694

#176
Pizzeria O'Scugnizzo
Cuisines: Pizza
Average Price: Inexpensive
Area: Palazzo Pitti
Address: Via Dell'orto 25R 50124
Florence Italy
Phone: 055 2286471

#177
Osteria Dell'agnolo
Cuisines: Italian, Steakhouses, Pizza
Average Price: Modest
Area: Santa Maria
Address: Via Borgo San Lorenzo 24R 50123
Florence Italy
Phone: 055 285923

#178
Osteria Hiron
Cuisines: Seafood
Average Price: Expensive
Area: Gavinana
Address: Via Lapo Da Castiglionchio 12R
50126
Florence Italy
Phone: 055 6581047

#179
Vecchio Carlino
Cuisines: Italian, Pizza
Average Price: Inexpensive
Area: Stazione Ferroviaria Santa Maria
Address: Viale Fratelli Rosselli 15 50144
Florence Italy
Phone: 055 353678

#180
Simbiosi
Cuisines: Pizza
Average Price: Modest
Area: Santa Maria
Address: Via Dè Ginori 56R 50123
Florence Italy
Phone: 055 0640115

#181
Gattabuia
Cuisines: Pizza, Italian
Average Price: Expensive
Area: Michelangelo
Address: Lungarno Cellini 13 50125
Florence Italy
Phone: 055 6814449

#182
Neromo
Cuisines: Italian
Average Price: Expensive
Area: Palazzo Pitti
Address: Borgo San Frediano 23 50124
Florence Italy
Phone: 055 2382645

#183
Io-Osteria Personale
Cuisines: Italian
Average Price: Exclusive
Area: Palazzo Pitti
Address: Borgo SAN Frediano, 167/R 50124
Florence Italy
Phone: 055 9331341

#184
Osteria I' Tozzo Di Pane
Cuisines: Italian
Average Price: Modest
Area: Indipendenza
Address: Via Guelfa 94R 50129
Florence Italy
Phone: 055 475753

#185
All'Antico Ristoro Di' Cambi
Cuisines: Tuscan
Average Price: Expensive
Area: Palazzo Pitti
Address: Via Sant'Onofrio 1R 50124
Florence Italy
Phone: 055 217134

#186
La Bottega Del Buon Caffè
Cuisines: Tuscan, Wine Bars
Average Price: Exclusive
Area: Michelangelo
Address: Lungarno Benvenuto Cellini
Florence Italy
Phone: 055 5535677

#187
Il Desco Bistrot
Cuisines: Gluten-Free,
Organic Stores, Vegetarian
Average Price: Modest
Area: Santa Maria
Address: Via Cavour 27 50129
Florence Italy
Phone: 055 288330

#188
Osteria Il Mostrino
Cuisines: Italian
Average Price: Modest
Area: Santa Maria
Address: Via Borgo Ognissanti 141R 50123
Florence Italy
Phone: 055 2398704

#189
Trattoria Borgo Antico
Cuisines: Pizza, Tuscan
Average Price: Modest
Area: Palazzo Pitti
Address: Piazza Santo Spirito 6R 50125
Florence Italy
Phone: 055 210437

#190
Sant' Ambrogio
Cuisines: Italian
Average Price: Expensive
Area: Santa Croce
Address: Via Luigi Carlo Farini 5R 50121
Florence Italy
Phone: 055 2469315

#191
Pane E Olio
Cuisines: Italian, Seafood, Live/Raw Food
Average Price: Exclusive
Area: Piazza Della Liberta/Savonarola
Address: Via Faentina 2 50133
Florence Italy
Phone: 055 488381

#192
Trattoria La Madia
Cuisines: Italian
Average Price: Modest
Area: Santa Maria
Address: Via Dell'alloro 11 50123
Florence Italy
Phone: 055 218563

#193
Haveli
Cuisines: Indian
Average Price: Modest
Area: Stazione Ferroviaria Santa Maria
Address: Viale Fratelli Rosselli 33R 50144
Florence Italy
Phone: 055 355695

#194
Le Barrique
Cuisines: Italian
Average Price: Expensive
Area: Palazzo Pitti
Address: Via Del Leone 40R 50124
Florence Italy
Phone: 055 224192

#195
Trattoria Sabatino
Cuisines: Tuscan
Average Price: Modest
Area: Palazzo Pitti
Address: Via Pisana 2R 50143
Florence Italy
Phone: 055 225955

#196
Mamma Napoli
Cuisines: Italian, Pizza
Average Price: Modest
Area: Santa Maria
Address: Piazza Dell Mercato Centrale 17R
50123 Florence Italy
Phone: 055 2052507

#197
Trattoria Sant'agostino
Cuisines: Tuscan, Trattorie
Average Price: Modest
Area: Palazzo Pitti
Address: Via Sant'agostino 23R 50100
Florence Italy
Phone: 055 210208

#198
Il Re Matto
Cuisines: Pizza, Italian
Average Price: Expensive
Area: Piazza Della Liberta/Savonarola,
Campo Di Marte
Address: Viale Dei Mille 152 50131
Florence Italy
Phone: 055 583851

#199
Odeon Bistro
Cuisines: Italian, Cocktail Bars, Wine Bars
Average Price: Modest
Area: Duomo
Address: Piazza Strozzi 8R 50123
Florence Italy
Phone: 055 215654

#200
l'Mangiarino
Cuisines: Italian
Average Price: Modest
Area: Duomo
Address: Via Dello Studio 5R 50122
Florence Italy
Phone: 055 216208

#201
Da Que' Ganzi
Cuisines: Tuscan, Seafood, Steakhouses
Average Price: Modest
Area: Santa Croce
Address: Via Ghibellina 70R 50122
Florence Italy
Phone: 055 2260010

#202
Pizza Man
Cuisines: Pizza
Average Price: Modest
Area: Campo Di Marte
Address: Viale De Amicis 47R 50137
Florence Italy
Phone: 055 0510049

#203
Osteria De' Peccatori
Cuisines: Pizza, Tuscan
Average Price: Modest
Area: Duomo
Address: Piazza San Firenze 14R 50122
Florence Italy
Phone: 055 287462

#204
Fiaschetteria Nuvoli
Cuisines: Beer, Wine & Spirits, Tuscan
Average Price: Modest
Area: Duomo
Address: Piazza Dell'olio 15 50123
Florence Italy
Phone: 055 2396616

#205
Jail House Live Music And Grill
Cuisines: Steakhouses, Italian
Average Price: Modest
Area: Novoli
Address: Via Della Villa Demidoff 92 50127
Florence Italy
Phone: 055 9335485

#206
Edi House
Cuisines: Italian
Average Price: Modest
Area: Piazza Della Liberta/Savonarola
Address: Piazza Fra' Girolamo Savonarola
9R 50132
Florence Italy
Phone: 055 588886

#207
Il Panda
Cuisines: Chinese, Food Delivery Services
Average Price: Inexpensive
Area: Piazza Della Liberta/Savonarola
Address: Via Fra' Bartolommeo 58 50132
Florence Italy
Phone: 055 573876

#208
I Templari
Cuisines: Tuscan
Average Price: Expensive
Area: Le Cascine
Address: Via Del Ponte Alle Mosse 132A
50144 Florence Italy
Phone: 055 355351

#209
Da Gherardo
Cuisines: Pizza
Average Price: Modest
Area: Palazzo Pitti
Address: Borgo San Frediano 57R 50124
Florence Italy
Phone: 055 282921

#210
Golden View Open Bar
Cuisines: Italian, Cafes
Average Price: Expensive
Area: Palazzo Pitti
Address: Via Dei Bardi 58R 50125
Florence Italy
Phone: 055 214502

#211
Hokkaido
Cuisines: Japanese, Sushi Bars
Average Price: Expensive
Area: Fortezza Basso
Address: Via Dello Statuto 21A 50129
Florence Italy
Phone: 055 494393

#212
Trattoria Cucchietta
Cuisines: Italian
Average Price: Modest
Area: Piazza Della Liberta/Savonarola
Address: Via Firenzuola Agnolo 15R 50133
Florence Italy
Phone: 055 578889

#213
Panini Toscani
Cuisines: Sandwiches
Average Price: Inexpensive
Area: Duomo
Address: Piazza Del Duomo 34R 50122
Florence Italy
Phone: 347 0043391

#214
Dim Sum
Cuisines: Dim Sum
Average Price: Modest
Area: Duomo
Address: Via Dei Neri 37R 50122
Florence Italy
Phone: 055 284331

#215
On Sapore Della Corea
Cuisines: Korean, Asian Fusion
Average Price: Modest
Area: Santa Maria
Address: Via Nazionale 73R 50123
Florence Italy
Phone: 334 8782450

#216
Fishing Lab Alle Murate
Cuisines: Seafood, Lounges, Live/Raw Food
Average Price: Modest
Area: Duomo
Address: Via Del Proconsolo 16R 50122
Florence Italy
Phone: 055 240618

#217
Caffetteria Piansa
Cuisines: Bars, Cafeteria
Average Price: Inexpensive
Area: Oberdan
Address: Via Gioberti 51R 50121
Florence Italy
Phone: 055 678015

#218
Palazzo Tempi
Cuisines: Italian, Pizza
Average Price: Modest
Area: Palazzo Pitti
Address: Via De' Bardi 37 50125
Florence Italy
Phone: 055 2466949

#219
One Eyed Jack
Cuisines: Pubs, Burgers, Hot Dogs
Average Price: Inexpensive
Area: Palazzo Pitti
Address: Piazza Nazario Sauro 2R 50124
Florence Italy
Phone: 055 0944561

#220
Il Guscio
Cuisines: Italian
Average Price: Expensive
Area: Palazzo Pitti
Address: Via Dell'orto 49 50124
Florence Italy
Phone: 055 224421

#221
Quinoa
Cuisines: Gluten-Free, Burgers, Thai
Average Price: Modest
Area: Duomo
Address: Vicolo Di Santa Maria Maggiore
Florence Italy
Phone: 055 290876

#222
La Galleria Il Vino Dei Guelfi
Cuisines: Pizza, Italian, Steakhouses
Average Price: Expensive
Area: Palazzo Pitti
Address: Via De' Guicciardini 48R 50125
Florence Italy
Phone: 055 2645988

#223
Il Forno 2000
Cuisines: Bakeries, Rotisserie Chicken
Average Price: Inexpensive
Area: Michelangelo
Address: Via Giampaolo Orsini 80R 50126
Florence Italy
Phone: 055 6801351

#224
Baccus
Cuisines: Italian
Average Price: Modest
Area: Santa Maria
Address: Borgo Ognissanti 45R 50123
Florence Italy
Phone: 055 283714

#225
La Spada
Cuisines: Italian
Average Price: Expensive
Area: Santa Maria
Address: Via Della Spada 62R 50123
Florence Italy
Phone: 055 218757

#226
Braciere Malatesta
Cuisines: Pizza, Steakhouses
Average Price: Modest
Area: Santa Maria
Address: Via Nazionale 36R 50123
Florence Italy
Phone: 055 215164

#227
Industria Ristorante
Cuisines: Mediterranean, Italian
Average Price: Modest
Area: Santa Maria
Address: Via Borgo Ognissanti 45R 50123
Florence Italy
Phone: 055 283714

#228
Banki Ramen
Cuisines: Ramen
Average Price: Modest
Area: Santa Maria
Address: Via Dei Banchi 14R 50123
Florence Italy
Phone: 055 213776

#229
Buca Poldo
Cuisines: Tuscan
Average Price: Modest
Area: Duomo
Address: Via Chiasso Degli Armagnati 2R
50122 Florence Italy
Phone: 055 2396578

#230
Tijuana
Cuisines: Mexican
Average Price: Modest
Area: Duomo
Address: Via Ghibellina 156R 50122
Florence Italy
Phone: 055 2341330

#231
Osteria Del Porcellino
Cuisines: Tuscan
Average Price: Modest
Area: Duomo
Address: Via Val Di Lamona 7R 50121
Florence Italy
Phone: 055 264148

#232
Chiosco Il Tempio
Cuisines: Bars, Cafes
Average Price: Inexpensive
Area: Oberdan
Address: Lungarno Del Tempio 1X 50126
Florence Italy
Phone: 333 3694137

#233
Scusate Il Ritardo
Cuisines: Pizza, Trattorie
Average Price: Modest
Area: Fortezza Basso
Address: Via Del Romito 51R 50134
Florence Italy
Phone: 331 4788538

#234
Arà
Cuisines: Sicilian, Ice Cream
Average Price: Inexpensive
Area: Duomo
Address: Via Degli Alfani 127 50121
Florence Italy
Phone: 333 1983927

#235
Osteria Dei Pazzi
Cuisines: Tuscan
Average Price: Modest
Area: Duomo
Address: Via Dei Lavatoi 1R 50122
Florence Italy
Phone: 055 2344880

#236
Trattoria Ponte Vecchio
Cuisines: Tuscan
Average Price: Expensive
Area: Duomo
Address: Lgarno Degli Archibusieri 8R 50122
Florence Italy
Phone: 055 292289

#237
Deliburger
Cuisines: Burgers
Average Price: Modest
Area: Novoli
Address: Via Carlo Del Prete 106D 50127
Florence Italy
Phone: 055 412462

#238
La Taverna Dei Matti
Cuisines: Pizza, Seafood
Average Price: Modest
Area: Campo Di Marte
Address: Piazza Di San Salvi 1 50135
Florence Italy
Phone: 055 666537

#239
Diladdarno
Cuisines: Italian
Average Price: Expensive
Area: Palazzo Pitti
Address: Via De' Serragli 108R 50124
Florence Italy
Phone: 055 224917

#240
Enoteca Fiorentina
Cuisines: Italian, Beer, Wine & Spirits, Bistros
Average Price: Expensive
Area: Santa Croce
Address: Via Pietrapiana 11R 50121
Florence Italy
Phone: 055 3880177

#241
Totò
Cuisines: Italian
Average Price: Modest
Area: Duomo
Address: Borgo Santissimi Apostoli 6R 50121
Florence Italy
Phone: 055 212096

#242
Pizzeria Il Teatro
Cuisines: Italian, Pizza
Average Price: Modest
Area: Duomo
Address: Via Ghibellina 128R 50122
Florence Italy
Phone: 055 2466954

#243
Niwa
Cuisines: Japanese, Thai
Average Price: Expensive
Area: Stazione Ferroviaria Santa Maria
Address: Via Ponte Alle Mosse 16R 50144
Florence Italy
Phone: 055 355736

#244
Pasticceria Silvano E Valentino
Cuisines: Patisserie/Cake Shop, Italian
Average Price: Modest
Area: Novoli
Address: Via Paganini Niccolò 2 50127
Florence Italy
Phone: 055 419681

#245
Rose's
Cuisines: Italian, Bars
Average Price: Modest
Area: Santa Maria
Address: Via Del Parione 26R 50123
Florence Italy
Phone: 055 287090

#246
Signorvino
Cuisines: Italian, Beer,
Wine & Spirits, Wine Bars
Average Price: Modest
Area: Palazzo Pitti
Address: Via Dei Bardi 46R 50125
Florence Italy
Phone: 055 286258

#247
La Terrazza Del Principe
Cuisines: Italian
Average Price: Expensive
Area: Palazzo Pitti
Address: Viale Niccolò Machiavelli 10 50125
Florence Italy
Phone: 055 224104

#248
Leonardo Self-Service
Cuisines: Buffets, Italian
Average Price: Inexpensive
Area: Santa Maria
Address: Via De Pecori 11 50123
Florence Italy
Phone: 055 284446

#249
Vecchia Osteria Dal Nacchero
Cuisines: Tuscan
Average Price: Modest
Area: Gavinana
Address: Piazza Gavinana 4R 50126
Florence Italy
Phone: 055 6587058

#250
Passaguai
Cuisines: Tuscan
Average Price: Expensive
Area: Palazzo Pitti
Address: Borgo San Frediano 44R 50124
Florence Italy
Phone: 055 0944528

#251
Yellow Bar
Cuisines: Pizza
Average Price: Modest
Area: Duomo
Address: Via Del Proconsolo 39R 50122
Florence Italy
Phone: 055 211766

#252
La Riseria
Cuisines: Italian
Average Price: Expensive
Area: Campo Di Marte
Address: Viale Dei Mille 19R 50131
Florence Italy
Phone: 055 4089081

#253
Il Caminetto
Cuisines: Italian
Average Price: Expensive
Area: Duomo
Address: Via Dello Studio 34R 50122
Florence Italy
Phone: 055 2396274

#254
Pizzeria Tirabaralla
Cuisines: Pizza, Italian
Average Price: Modest
Area: Santa Maria
Address: Via Della Scalla 28 50123
Florence Italy
Phone: 055 218418

#255
La Leggenda Dei Frati
Cuisines: Italian
Average Price: Exclusive
Area: Michelangelo
Address: Costa San Giorgio 6A 50125
Florence Italy
Phone: 055 0680545

#256
L'Trippaio Fiorentino
Cuisines: Food Stands
Average Price: Inexpensive
Area: Oberdan
Address: Via Gioberti 133R 50121
Florence Italy
Phone: 335 8216880

#257
Gelateria Dei Neri
Cuisines: Ice Cream & Frozen Yogurt,
Creperies, Gelato
Average Price: Inexpensive
Area: Duomo
Address: Via Dei Neri 9 50122
Florence Italy
Phone: 055 210034

#258
I Tarocchi
Cuisines: Pizza, Italian
Average Price: Modest
Area: Michelangelo
Address: Via Dei Renai 12R 50100
Florence Italy
Phone: 055 2343912

#259
Enoteca Pinchiorri
Cuisines: Italian
Average Price: Exclusive
Area: Duomo
Address: Via Ghibellina 87 50122
Florence Italy
Phone: 055 242777

#260
Il Barroccio
Cuisines: Italian
Average Price: Modest
Area: Duomo
Address: Via Vigna Vecchia 31R 50100
Florence Italy
Phone: 055 6271019

#261
Lobs Fish
Cuisines: Italian, Vegetarian, Seafood
Average Price: Expensive
Area: Santa Maria
Address: Via Faenza 75R 50123
Florence Italy
Phone: 055 212478

#262
l'cchè C'è C'è
Cuisines: Tuscan, Trattorie
Average Price: Expensive
Area: Duomo
Address: Via Magalotti 11R 50122
Florence Italy
Phone: 055 216589

#263
Cicalone Osteria & Vinaino
Cuisines: Mediterranean, Italian
Average Price: Modest
Area: Santa Maria, Duomo
Address: Via Delle Belle Donne 43R 50123
Florence Italy
Phone: 055 215492

#264
Giannino In San Lorenzo
Cuisines: Italian
Average Price: Modest
Area: Duomo
Address: Borgo San Lorenzo 13 50123
Florence Italy
Phone: 055 2399799

#265
Trattoria Il Bargello
Cuisines: Italian
Average Price: Modest
Area: Duomo
Address: Borgo Dè Greci 37R 50122
Florence Italy
Phone: 055 218605

#266
l'tosto
Cuisines: Sandwiches, Italian, Food Stands
Average Price: Inexpensive
Area: Duomo
Address: Via Dei Servi 8 R 50121
Florence Italy
Phone: 055 0515280

#267
Due Sorsi & Un Boccone
Cuisines: Creperies, Beer,
Wine & Spirits, Sandwiches
Average Price: Inexpensive
Area: Duomo
Address: Via Degli Alfani 105R 50121
Florence Italy
Phone: 334 2640931

#268
La Lola
Cuisines: Trattorie
Average Price: Modest
Area: Palazzo Pitti
Address: Via Della Chiesa 16R 50125
Florence Italy
Phone: 055 2654254

#269
l'Pizzacchiere
Cuisines: Pizza
Average Price: Inexpensive
Area: Michelangelo
Address: Via San Miniato 2 50125
Florence Italy
Phone: 055 2466332

#270
Pizza Napoli 1955
Cuisines: Pizza
Average Price: Modest
Area: Duomo
Address: Via Dei Neri 73 50122
Florence Italy
Phone: 055 287815

#271
Francesco Vini
Cuisines: Tuscan, Wine Bars
Average Price: Expensive
Area: Duomo
Address: Borgo Dei Greci 7R 50122
Florence Italy
Phone: 055 218737

#272
La Divina Pizza
Cuisines: Pizza, Vegetarian
Average Price: Inexpensive
Area: Santa Croce
Address: Via Borgo Allegri 50R 50122
Florence Italy
Phone: 055 2347498

#273
Buca Lapi
Cuisines: Tuscan
Average Price: Expensive
Area: Duomo
Address: Via Del Trebbio 1 50123
Florence Italy
Phone: 055 213768

#274
Il Giardino Di Barbano
Cuisines: Pizza, Italian
Average Price: Modest
Area: Indipendenza
Address: Piazza Indipendenza 3 50129
Florence Italy
Phone: 055 486752

#275
Trattoria l'Raddi
Cuisines: Tuscan
Average Price: Expensive
Area: Palazzo Pitti
Address: Via d'Ardiglione 47R 50125
Florence Italy
Phone: 055 211072

#276
Gecko
Cuisines: Steakhouses, Tapas Bars
Average Price: Modest
Area: Michelangelo
Address: Via Dei Renai 11 50125
Florence Italy
Phone: 342 0350297

#277
La Bottega Del Pizzaiolo
Cuisines: Pizza
Average Price: Inexpensive
Area: Campo Di Marte
Address: Via Franceschi Ferrucci Caterina 46
50135 Florence Italy
Phone: 055 609696

#278
L'Pappagallo
Cuisines: Bars, Patisserie,
Cake Shop, Cafeteria
Average Price: Modest
Area: Oberdan
Address: Via Fra Giovanni Angelico 7R
50121 Florence Italy
Phone: 055 670525

#279
Olio Restaurant
Cuisines: Italian
Average Price: Expensive
Area: Palazzo Pitti
Address: Via Santo Spirito 4 50125
Florence Italy
Phone: 055 2658198

#280
Il Cavaliere
Cuisines: Italian
Average Price: Expensive
Area: Indipendenza
Address: Viale Lavagnini Spartaco 22 50129
Florence Italy
Phone: 055 471914

#281
La Carabaccia
Cuisines: Tuscan, Trattorie, Pizza
Average Price: Expensive
Area: Stazione Ferroviaria Santa Maria
Address: Via Palazzuolo 190R 50123
Florence Italy
Phone: 055 214782

#282
Vineria Panineria Scheggi
Cuisines: Tuscan, Sandwiches
Average Price: Modest
Area: Campo Di Marte
Address: Viale Dei Mille 1C 50131
Florence Italy
Phone: 055 588076

#283
Oliandolo
Cuisines: Italian
Average Price: Modest
Area: Duomo
Address: Via Ricasoli 38R 50122
Florence Italy
Phone: 055 211296

#284
Eby's Latin
Cuisines: Mexican, Lounges
Average Price: Inexpensive
Area: Duomo
Address: Via Dell'oriuolo 5R 50125
Florence Italy
Phone: 055 2477653

#285
Wasabi Kaiten Sushi
Cuisines: Japanese, Sushi Bars, Buffets
Average Price: Modest
Area: Santa Maria
Address: Via Dè Ginori 20R 50129
Florence Italy
Phone: 055 283065

#286
Enzo & Piero
Cuisines: Italian
Average Price: Expensive
Area: Santa Maria
Address: Via Faena 105R 50123
Florence Italy
Phone: 055 214901

#287
Ballerini
Cuisines: Chocolatiers & Shops,
Patisserie/Cake Shop, Bistros
Average Price: Modest
Area: Stazione Ferroviaria Santa Maria
Address: Borgo Ognissanti 132R 50123
Florence Italy
Phone: 055 215094

#288
Gustaosteria
Cuisines: Italian
Average Price: Modest
Area: Palazzo Pitti
Address: Via De' Michelozzi 13R 50125
Florence Italy
Phone: 055 285033

#289
Obicà
Cuisines: Pizza, Italian
Average Price: Expensive
Area: Duomo
Address: Via De Tornabuoni 16 50123
Florence Italy
Phone: 055 2773526

#290
Pandemonio
Cuisines: Tuscan
Average Price: Exclusive
Area: Palazzo Pitti
Address: Via Del Leone 50R 50124
Florence Italy
Phone: 055 224002

#291
Osteria De L'Ortolano
Cuisines: Tuscan
Average Price: Modest
Area: Duomo
Address: Via Degli Alfani 91R 50121
Florence Italy
Phone: 055 2396466

#292
Fuor D'acqua
Cuisines: Seafood, Italian
Average Price: Exclusive
Area: Palazzo Pitti
Address: Via Pisana 37R 50143
Florence Italy
Phone: 055 222299

#293
Senza Nome
Cuisines: Pizza
Average Price: Modest
Area: Le Cascine
Address: Via Doni 43 50144
Florence Italy
Phone: 055 350696

#294
Santarpia
Cuisines: Pizza, Gluten-Free
Average Price: Modest
Area: Santa Croce
Address: Largo Annigoni 9C 50122
Florence Italy
Phone: 055 245829

#295
Trattoria Dall'oste
Cuisines: Tuscan, Seafood, Steakhouses
Average Price: Expensive
Area: Stazione Ferroviaria Santa Maria
Address: Via Luigi Alamanni 3R 50123
Florence Italy
Phone: 055 212048

#296
Gosh
Cuisines: Italian, Cocktail Bars
Average Price: Inexpensive
Area: Palazzo Pitti
Address: Via Santo Spirito 46R 50125
Florence Italy
Phone: 055 0469048

#297
Boccanegra
Cuisines: Italian
Average Price: Modest
Area: Duomo
Address: Via Ghibellina 124R 50122
Florence Italy
Phone: 055 2001098

#298
Dinastia Tang
Cuisines: Chinese, Fast Food
Average Price: Inexpensive
Area: Indipendenza
Address: Via San Zanobi 2R 50129
Florence Italy
Phone: 055 285390

#299
Il Barrino
Cuisines: Tuscan
Average Price: Expensive
Area: Oberdan
Address: Via Gioberti Vincenzo 71R 50121
Florence Italy
Phone: 055 660565

#300
Ditta Artigianale
Cuisines: Cafeteria, Cafes, Italian
Average Price: Inexpensive
Area: Palazzo Pitti
Address: Via Dello Sprone 3R 50125
Florence Italy
Phone: 055 2741541

#301
Cucineria La Mattonaia
Cuisines: Italian, Modern European
Average Price: Expensive
Area: Santa Croce
Address: Via Della Mattonaia 19R 50121
Florence Italy
Phone: 055 3860564

#302
Gesto
Cuisines: Cafes, Bistros, Tapas Bars
Average Price: Modest
Area: Palazzo Pitti
Address: Borgo San Frediano 27R
Florence, Firenze Italy
Phone: 393 9540021

#303
Lo Stravagante
Cuisines: Italian
Average Price: Expensive
Area: Piazza Della Liberta/Savonarola
Address: Via Boccaccio Giovanni 35R 50133
Florence Italy
Phone: 055 5048137

#304
Ai Lungarni
Cuisines: Italian, Pizza, Sandwiches
Average Price: Inexpensive
Area: Santa Maria
Address: Lungarno Vespucci 14R 50123
Florence Italy
Phone: 055 2670236

#305
Paoli
Cuisines: Tuscan
Average Price: Modest
Area: Duomo
Address: Via Dei Tavolini 12R 50122
Florence Italy
Phone: 055 216215

#306
Il Boccale
Cuisines: Italian
Average Price: Modest
Area: Duomo
Address: Borgo Santi Apostoli 33 50123
Florence Italy
Phone: 055 283384

#307
College House
Cuisines: Cafeteria, Cafes,
Breakfast & Brunch
Average Price: Inexpensive
Area: Novoli
Address: Via Cammeo 50127
Florence Italy
Phone: 340 0047365

#308
Frescobaldi
Cuisines: Italian, Wine Bars
Average Price: Expensive
Area: Duomo
Address: Via Dei Magazzini 4R 50122
Florence Italy
Phone: 055 284724

#309
Acqua Al 2
Cuisines: Tuscan
Average Price: Modest
Area: Duomo
Address: Via Della Vigna Vecchia 40R 50122
Florence Italy
Phone: 055 284170

#310
I' Pennatini
Cuisines: Italian
Average Price: Modest
Area: Monticelli
Address: Via Giovanni Della Casa 6 50143
Florence Italy
Phone: 055 701466

#311
La Mangiatoia
Cuisines: Italian
Average Price: Modest
Area: Palazzo Pitti
Address: Piazza San Felice 8R 50125
Florence Italy
Phone: 055 224060

#312
L'Altra Piadineria
Cuisines: Sandwiches
Average Price: Inexpensive
Area: Monticelli
Address: Via Del Sansovino 2B 50142
Florence Italy
Phone: 055 7390389

#313
Vagalume
Cuisines: Italian
Average Price: Modest
Area: Santa Croce
Address: Via Pietrapiana 40R 50122
Florence Italy
Phone: 055 2466740

#314
Santa Felicita
Cuisines: Italian, Pizza
Average Price: Modest
Area: Palazzo Pitti
Address: Piazza Santa Felicita 6R 50014
Firenze Italy
Phone: 055 284495

#315
Fulin
Cuisines: Chinese
Average Price: Expensive
Area: Michelangelo
Address: Via Giampaolo Orsini 113 50125
Florence Italy
Phone: 055 684931

#316
Club Del Gusto
Cuisines: Fast Food
Average Price: Inexpensive
Area: Duomo
Address: Via Dei Neri 50R 50122
Florence Italy
Phone: 348 0903142

#317
Il Ristoro Dei Perditempo
Cuisines: Wine Bars, Italian
Average Price: Exclusive
Area: Palazzo Pitti
Address: Borgo San Iacopo 48R 50125
Florence Italy
Phone: 055 2645569

#318
Mister Pizza
Cuisines: Pizza, Italian
Average Price: Inexpensive
Area: Duomo
Address: Piazza Del Duomo 5R 50122
Florence Italy
Phone: 055 2382263

#319
L'Officina Ferrucci
Cuisines: Cafes, Coffee & Tea, Italian
Average Price: Inexpensive
Area: Michelangelo
Address: Via Giampaolo Orsini 125R 50125
Florence Italy
Phone: 055 687788

#320
Al Noor
Cuisines: Indian, Kebab
Average Price: Inexpensive
Area: Santa Croce
Address: Borgo La Croce 20R 50121
Florence Italy
Phone: 055 0516183

#321
Cloud 59
Cuisines: Burgers, Sandwiches, Wine Bars
Average Price: Modest
Area: Santa Maria
Address: Via Dè Ginori 59R 50123
Florence Italy
Phone: 344 1373187

#322
Ristorante Sabatini
Cuisines: Italian
Average Price: Expensive
Area: Santa Maria
Address: Via Panzani, 9r 50123
Florence Italy
Phone: 055 282802

#323
Trattoria Cammillo
Cuisines: Italian
Average Price: Expensive
Area: Palazzo Pitti
Address: Borgo San Iacopo 57R 50125
Florence Italy
Phone: 055 212427

#324
Piazza Del Vino
Cuisines: Wine Bars, Italian
Average Price: Expensive
Area: Campo Di Marte
Address: Via Della Torretta 18R 50137
Florence Italy
Phone: 055 671404

#325
Gandhi
Cuisines: Indian
Average Price: Modest
Area: Stazione Ferroviaria Santa Maria
Address: Via Il Prato 38R 50123
Florence Italy
Phone: 055 2654474

#326
La Dantesca
Cuisines: Italian, Pizza
Average Price: Modest
Area: Santa Maria
Address: Via Panzani 57R 50123
Florence Italy
Phone: 055 212287

#327
Paninoteca Li Per Lì
Cuisines: Sandwiches
Average Price: Inexpensive
Area: Indipendenza
Address: Via 27 Aprile 42R 50129
Florence Italy
Phone: 393 8083449

#328
Speakeasy 23
Cuisines: Wine Bars, Bistros
Average Price: Modest
Area: Michelangelo
Address: Via San Niccolo 23R 50125
Florence Italy
Phone: 055 2346502

#329
Come Dio Comanda
Cuisines: Sandwiches
Average Price: Inexpensive
Area: Michelangelo
Address: Via San Nicolo 69R 50125
Florence Italy
Phone: 338 4729299

#330
Osteria Del Proconsolo
Cuisines: Tuscan, Pizza
Average Price: Modest
Area: Duomo
Address: Via Del Proconsolo 59R 50122
Florence Italy
Phone: 055 213069

#331
Antica Friggitoria Dell'albero
Cuisines: Pizza, Friterie
Average Price: Inexpensive
Area: Santa Maria
Address: Via Dell'albero 16R 50123
Florence Italy
Phone: 334 9098907

#332
Alas
Cuisines: Greek
Average Price: Modest
Area: Duomo
Address: Via Camillo Benso Cavour
Florence Italy
Phone: 055 268059

#333
Rosticceria Giuliano
Cuisines: Steakhouses
Average Price: Modest
Area: Gavinana
Address: Via Giovanni Dalle Bande Nere 38
50126 Florence Italy
Phone: 055 680741

#334
La Farmacia Dei Sani
Cuisines: Wine Bars, Sandwiches
Average Price: Inexpensive
Area: Fortezza Basso
Address: Piazza Giorgini 7A 50134
Florence Italy
Phone: 055 481572

#335
Caffè Cibrèo
Cuisines: Italian
Average Price: Expensive
Area: Santa Croce
Address: Via Del Verrocchio 5R 50122
Florence Italy
Phone: 055 2345853

#336
Taverna Degli Artisti
Cuisines: Pizza
Average Price: Inexpensive
Area: Piazza Della Liberta/Savonarola
Address: Via Degli Artisti 20R 50132
Florence Italy
Phone: 055 0465022

#337
La Cocotte
Cuisines: Cafes, Steakhouses, Tuscan
Average Price: Modest
Area: Santa Maria
Address: Via Nazionale 112R 50123
Florence Italy
Phone: 055 283114

#338
Cibrèo
Cuisines: Tuscan
Average Price: Exclusive
Area: Santa Croce
Address: Via Andrea Del Verrocchio
Florence Italy
Phone: 055 2341100

#339
San Gallo
Cuisines: Pizza, Italian
Average Price: Modest
Area: Indipendenza
Address: Via San Gallo 4R 50129
Florence Italy
Phone: 055 2399893

#340
Pizza Man
Cuisines: Pizza
Average Price: Modest
Area: Novoli
Address: Via Carlo Del Prete 10R 50127
Florence Italy
Phone: 055 433849

#341
Itacho Sushi
Cuisines: Japanese, Thai, Chinese
Average Price: Modest
Area: Le Cascine
Address: Via Ponte Alle Mosse 9 50144
Florence Italy
Phone: 055 355061

#342
Cuco
Cuisines: Italian
Average Price: Modest
Area: Santa Maria
Address: Via Del Melarancio 4R 50123
Florence Italy
Phone: 347 5217260

#343
La Cucina Del Ghianda
Cuisines: Tuscan, Mediterranean
Average Price: Expensive
Area: Santa Croce
Address: Via Dell'agnolo 85R 50122
Florence Italy
Phone: 055 3860534

#344
La Pergola
Cuisines: Breakfast & Brunch, Cafes
Average Price: Modest
Area: Duomo
Address: Via Della Pergola 23 50121
Florence Italy
Phone: 055 7301453

#345
Filipepe
Cuisines: Italian, Seafood
Average Price: Expensive
Area: Michelangelo
Address: Via San Niccolò 39R 50125
Florence Italy
Phone: 055 2001397

#346
Pizzeria La Porta Verde
Cuisines: Pizza
Average Price: Modest
Area: Campo Di Marte
Address: Via D'orso Antonio 7R 50135
Florence Italy
Phone: 055 606345

#347
Antica Porta
Cuisines: Pizza
Average Price: Modest
Area: Palazzo Pitti
Address: Via Senese 23R 50124
Florence Italy
Phone: 055 220527

#348
Iyo Iyo
Cuisines: Sushi Bars, Japanese
Average Price: Modest
Area: Duomo
Address: Borgo Pinti 25R 50121
Florence Italy
Phone: 338 7653069

#349
Touch Florence
Cuisines: Tuscan
Average Price: Expensive
Area: Santa Croce
Address: Via Di Mezzo 42R 50121
Florence Italy
Phone: 055 2466150

#350
Arnold's Firenze
Cuisines: Burgers
Average Price: Inexpensive
Area: Stazione Ferroviaria Santa Maria
Address: Piazzale Porta Al Prato 47 50123
Florence Italy
Phone: 327 7870231

#351
Sandwichic
Cuisines: Sandwiches
Average Price: Inexpensive
Area: Indipendenza
Address: Via San Gallo 3R 50129
Florence Italy
Phone: 055 281157

#352
Hoseki
Cuisines: Japanese
Average Price: Expensive
Area: Stazione Ferroviaria Santa Maria
Address: Via Il Prato 66R 50123
Florence Italy
Phone: 055 282012

#353
La Tana Di' Gatto
Cuisines: Bars, Italian
Average Price: Inexpensive
Area: Palazzo Pitti
Address: Via Sant'agostino 12R 50125
Florence Italy
Phone: 055 0453163

#354
Ristorante Alla Griglia
Cuisines: Italian
Average Price: Expensive
Area: Santa Maria
Address: Via Dei Banchi 25R 50123
Florence Italy
Phone: 055 290314

#355
Enoteca Fuori Porta
Cuisines: Tuscan, Bars
Average Price: Modest
Area: Michelangelo
Address: Via Del Monte Alle Croci 10 50125
Florence Italy
Phone: 055 2342483

#356
Osteria Cipolla Rossa
Cuisines: Italian
Average Price: Expensive
Area: Santa Maria
Address: Via Dè Conti 53 50123
Florence Italy
Phone: 055 214210

#357
Trattoria Katti
Cuisines: Tuscan
Average Price: Modest
Area: Santa Maria
Address: Via Faenza 31R 50123
Florence Italy
Phone: 055 219305

#358
Bamboo Sushi-Wok
Cuisines: Chinese, Sushi Bars, Italian
Average Price: Modest
Area: Novoli
Address: Via Di Novoli 53 50127
Florence Italy
Phone: 055 414852

#359
The Bench Caffe Gourmet
Cuisines: Cafeteria, Bistros, Lounges
Average Price: Inexpensive
Area: Duomo
Address: Via Dei Servi 91R
Florence, Firenze Italy
Phone: 055 2657504

#360
Trattoria Lo Stracotto
Cuisines: Italian, Wine Bars
Average Price: Modest
Area: Santa Maria
Address: Piazza Madonna Degli Aldobrandini
16 50123 Florence Italy
Phone: 055 2302062

#361
Il Piacere
Cuisines: Italian
Average Price: Expensive
Area: Campo Di Marte
Address: Via Gabriele D'Annunzio 149 50135
Florence Italy
Phone: 055 602605

#362
Lo Scudo
Cuisines: Italian, Mediterranean, Pizza
Average Price: Modest
Area: Duomo
Address: Via Dell'Oriuolo 53R 50122
Florence Italy
Phone: 055 284495

#363
Club Culinario Toscano Da Osvaldo
Cuisines: Italian
Average Price: Expensive
Area: Duomo
Address: Piazza De Peruzzi 3 50122
Florence Italy
Phone: 055 217919

#364
Amici Di Ponte Vecchio
Cuisines: Italian, Pizza, Sandwiches
Average Price: Inexpensive
Area: Palazzo Pitti
Address: Via Dei Bardi 39 50125
Florence Italy
Phone: 055 285301

#365
Firenze Nova
Cuisines: Pizza, Seafood
Average Price: Expensive
Area: Novoli
Address: Via Benedetto Dei 94 50127
Florence Italy
Phone: 055 411937

#366
Konnubio
Cuisines: Vegan, Tuscan,
Breakfast & Brunch
Average Price: Expensive
Area: Santa Maria
Address: Via Dei Conti 8R 50123
Florence Italy
Phone: 055 2381189

#367
Lungarno Bistrot
Cuisines: Italian, Bistros, Mediterranean
Average Price: Exclusive
Area: Palazzo Pitti
Address: Piazza Degli Scarlatti 1R 50125
Florence Italy
Phone: 055 2654541

#368
Mama's Bakery
Cuisines: Bakeries, Breakfast & Brunch,
Patisserie/Cake Shop
Average Price: Modest
Area: Palazzo Pitti
Address: Via Della Chiesa 34R 50125
Florence Italy
Phone: 055 219214

#369
Winter Garden By Caino
Cuisines: Italian
Average Price: Exclusive
Area: Santa Maria
Address: Piazza D'ognissanti 1 50123
Florence Italy
Phone: 055 27163770

#370
Il Mandarino
Cuisines: Chinese
Average Price: Modest
Area: Duomo
Address: Via Della Condotta 17R 50122
Florence Italy
Phone: 055 2396130

#371
Berberè
Cuisines: Pizza, Beer Gardens
Average Price: Modest
Area: Palazzo Pitti
Address: Piazza De Nerli 1 50124
Florence Italy
Phone: 055 2382946

#372
Trattoria Da Ginone
Cuisines: Tuscan
Average Price: Modest
Area: Palazzo Pitti
Address: Via De' Serragli 35R 50124
Florence Italy
Phone: 055 218758

#373
Foody Farm
Cuisines: Fast Food, Cocktail Bars
Average Price: Modest
Area: Santa Croce
Address: Corso Dei Tintori 10R 50122
Florence Italy
Phone: 055 242327

#374
La Luna Nuova
Cuisines: Restaurants
Average Price: Modest
Area: Oberdan
Address: Via Gioberti Vincenzo, 93R 50121
Florence Italy
Phone: 055 663810

#375
Lo Skipper Club
Cuisines: Seafood, Sicilian
Average Price: Expensive
Area: Duomo
Address: Via Degli Alfani 78R 50121
Florence Italy
Phone: 055 284019

#376
Belcore
Cuisines: Italian
Average Price: Expensive
Area: Santa Maria
Address: Via Dell'albero 30 50123
Florence Italy
Phone: 055 211198

#377
Le Vespe Cafe
Cuisines: Diners, Breakfast & Brunch, Cafes
Average Price: Modest
Area: Santa Croce
Address: Via Ghibellina 76R 50122
Florence Italy
Phone: 055 3880062

#378
#Raw
Cuisines: Live/Raw Food, Vegan, Vegetarian
Average Price: Inexpensive
Area: Palazzo Pitti
Address: Via Sant'Agostino 11R 50125
Florence Italy
Phone: 055 219379

#379
Gusta Panino
Cuisines: Sandwiches, Italian
Average Price: Inexpensive
Area: Palazzo Pitti
Address: Via De Michelozzi 13R 50125
Florence Italy
Phone: 055 285033

#380
00 - Zerozero
Cuisines: Pizza, Italian
Average Price: Expensive
Area: Fortezza Basso
Address: Via Giovanni Lorenzoni 8R 50134
Florence Italy
Phone: 055 495000

#381
Affè Di Bacco
Cuisines: Pizza, Italian
Average Price: Modest
Area: Michelangelo
Address: Via Di Rusciano 16R 50126
Florence Italy
Phone: 055 6810109

#382
Vecchio Mercato
Cuisines: Tuscan
Average Price: Expensive
Area: Santa Maria
Address: Piazza Del Mercato Centrale 12R
50123 Florence Italy
Phone: 055 211978

#383
Tosca
Cuisines: Tuscan, Mediterranean
Average Price: Expensive
Area: Santa Maria
Address: Piazza Del Mercato Centrale 13
50123 Florence Italy
Phone: 055 2657424

#384
Tijuana Mexican Grill
Cuisines: Mexican
Average Price: Expensive
Area: Stazione Ferroviaria Santa Maria
Address: Via Il Prato 57 50123
Florence Italy
Phone: 055 287247

#385
Brandolino
Cuisines: Pizza, Tuscan
Average Price: Expensive
Area: Santa Maria
Address: Piazza Di Madonna Degli
Aldobrandini 3R 50123
Florence Italy
Phone: 055 3997593

#386
Drogheria
Cuisines: Burgers, Bars
Average Price: Expensive
Area: Santa Croce
Address: Piazza Annigoni 22 50122
Florence Italy
Phone: 055 2478869

#387
Pasticceria Renato
Cuisines: Desserts, Italian
Average Price: Modest
Area: Campo Di Marte
Address: Via Aretina 57C 50136
Florence Italy
Phone: 055 677391

#388
Caffe Rosano
Cuisines: Cafes, Italian
Average Price: Inexpensive
Area: Indipendenza
Address: Via San Gallo 29R 50129
Florence Italy
Phone: 338 1541315

#389
Bar Pasticceria Gaetano
Cuisines: Desserts, Cafes
Average Price: Modest
Area: Novoli
Address: Via Di Novoli 50127
Florence Italy
Phone: 055 411841

#390
Salumeria Verdi
Cuisines: Sandwiches, Salumerie
Average Price: Inexpensive
Area: Santa Croce
Address: Via Verdi Giuseppe 36R 50122
Florence Italy
Phone: 055 244517

#391
Il Faraone
Cuisines: Middle Eastern, Fast Food, Kebab
Average Price: Inexpensive
Area: Le Cascine
Address: Via Cristofori Bartolomeo, 14R
50144 Florence Italy
Phone: 055 366592

#392
The Opposite
Cuisines: Bistros
Average Price: Modest
Area: Novoli
Address: Palazzo Di Giustizia 50127
Florence Italy
Phone: 055 4377937

#393
Le Capelle Medicee
Cuisines: Italian
Average Price: Modest
Area: Santa Maria
Address: Via Canto Dei Nelli 30R 50123
Florence Italy
Phone: 055 6287005

#394
Moba
Cuisines: Italian
Average Price: Expensive
Area: Michelangelo
Address: Costa Di San Giorgio 4 50125
Florence Italy
Phone: 055 2008444

#395
Bella Blu
Cuisines: Cafes
Average Price: Modest
Area: Campo Di Marte
Address: Via Lungo L'Affrico 96R 50135
Florence Italy
Phone: 055 608652

#396
Burro&Acciughe
Cuisines: Bistros, Seafood
Average Price: Modest
Area: Palazzo Pitti
Address: Via Dell'orto 35R 50124
Florence Italy
Phone: 055 0457286

#397
Orcagna
Cuisines: Italian
Average Price: Modest
Area: Duomo
Address: Piazza Della Signoria 1R 50122
Florence Italy
Phone: 055 292188

#398
Trattoria Cibrèo - Cibrèino
Cuisines: Trattorie
Average Price: Expensive
Area: Santa Croce
Address: Via Dei Macci 122R 50122
Florence Italy
Phone: 055 2341100

#399
Cucina Torcicoda
Cuisines: Italian, Steakhouses, Pizza
Average Price: Expensive
Area: Duomo
Address: Via Torta 5R 50122
Florence Italy
Phone: 055 4691193

#400
Borgo San Jacopo
Cuisines: Italian
Average Price: Exclusive
Area: Palazzo Pitti
Address: Borgo San Jacopo 62R 50125
Florence Italy
Phone: 055 281661

#401
Il Magazzino
Cuisines: Tuscan, Trattorie
Average Price: Expensive
Area: Palazzo Pitti
Address: Piazza Della Passera 2 50125
Florence Italy
Phone: 055 215969

#402
JT Caffè
Cuisines: Wine Bars, Italian, Cocktail Bars
Average Price: Modest
Area: Palazzo Pitti
Address: Piazza Pitti 32R 50125
Florence Italy
Phone: 055 281143

#403
Cafe1926
Cuisines: French, Italian, Cafeteria
Average Price: Modest
Area: Santa Croce
Address: Via Giovan Battista Niccolini 30R
50121 Florence Italy
Phone: 055 2346296

#404
Club Paradiso
Cuisines: Italian
Average Price: Modest
Area: Palazzo Pitti
Address: Via Dell'orto 24 50124
Florence Italy
Phone: 055 223955

#405
Masterchips
Cuisines: Hot Dogs, Burgers, Friterie
Average Price: Inexpensive
Area: Santa Maria
Address: Via Nazionale 22 50123
Florence Italy
Phone: 081 19339082

#406
Il Piacere
Cuisines: Italian
Average Price: Inexpensive
Area: Campo Di Marte
Address: Via Mosciotti 1B 50131
Florence Italy
Phone: 055 05002806

#407
Paninopoli
Cuisines: Sandwiches
Average Price: Inexpensive
Area: Palazzo Pitti
Address: Via Romana, 40R 50125
Florence Italy
Phone: 055 224164

#408
Rivalta Caffè
Cuisines: Bars, Cafes
Average Price: Modest
Area: Santa Maria
Address: Via Lungarno Corsini 12R 50123
Florence Italy
Phone: 055 289810

#409
Oliviero
Cuisines: Tuscan
Average Price: Exclusive
Area: Duomo
Address: Via Delle Terme 51R 50123
Florence Italy
Phone: 055 212421

#410
Trattoria Le Cave Di Maiano
Cuisines: Tuscan, Gluten-Free, Trattorie
Average Price: Modest
Area: Bosco Bello
Address: Via Cave Di Maiano 16 50014
Fiesole Italy
Phone: 055 59133

#411
Trattoria Napoleone
Cuisines: Italian
Average Price: Expensive
Area: Palazzo Pitti
Address: Piazza Del Carmine 24 50124
Florence Italy
Phone: 055 281015

#412
Vinaino Fiorenza
Cuisines: Italian, Cafes
Average Price: Inexpensive
Area: Duomo
Address: Via Vacchereccia 13R 50122
Florence Italy
Phone: 055 2655847

#413
Trattoria Buzzino
Cuisines: Trattorie
Average Price: Modest
Area: Duomo
Address: Via Dei Leoni 8R 50122
Florence Italy
Phone: 055 2398013

#414
Lo Schiacciavino
Cuisines: Sandwiches, Wine Bars
Average Price: Inexpensive
Area: Santa Croce
Address: Via Giuseppe Verdi 6R 50122
Florence Italy
Phone: 055 2260133

#415
Vincanto
Cuisines: Tuscan, Pizza
Average Price: Expensive
Area: Santa Maria
Address: Piazza Santa Maria 29R 50123
Florence Italy
Phone: 393 4474744

#416
Da Fiaschino
Cuisines: Italian, Sandwiches, Wine Bars
Average Price: Inexpensive
Area: Duomo
Address: Via Sant'egidio 3R 50122
Florence Italy
Phone: 348 6605010

#417
La Cambusa Del Capitano
Cuisines: Seafood, Italian
Average Price: Expensive
Area: Novoli
Address: Viale Corsica 31R 50127
Florence Italy
Phone: 055 3992053

#418
La Botteghina Di Daniele
Cuisines: Pizza
Average Price: Inexpensive
Area: Campo Di Marte
Address: V.Le Fanti Manfredo, 125/A 50137
Florence Italy
Phone: 055 600666

#419
Pastation
Cuisines: Italian, Cafeteria, Pasta Shops
Average Price: Modest
Area: Duomo
Address: Via Porta Rossa 64 50123
Florence Italy
Phone: 055 291184

#420
Florian
Cuisines: Cafes, Breakfast & Brunch
Average Price: Expensive
Area: Santa Maria
Address: Via Del Parione 32R 50123
Florence Italy
Phone: 055 284291

#421
Pizzeria Riva d'Arno
Cuisines: Pizza
Average Price: Modest
Area: Palazzo Pitti
Address: Lungarno Soderini 7R 50124
Florence Italy
Phone: 055 280223

#422
Tato
Cuisines: Tuscan, Cocktail Bars, Pizza
Average Price: Expensive
Area: Santa Croce
Address: Largo Piero Bargellini 2 50122
Florence Italy
Phone: 055 2638701

#423
Grand Hotel Baglioni
Cuisines: Hotels, Bars, Italian
Average Price: Expensive
Area: Santa Maria
Address: Piazza Dell'unità Italiana 6 50123
Florence Italy
Phone: 055 23580

#424
Da Mimmo
Cuisines: Italian
Average Price: Expensive
Area: Indipendenza
Address: Via San Gallo, 57-59 R 50129
Florence Italy
Phone: 055 481030

#425
Truffle Experience
Cuisines: Tuscan
Average Price: Expensive
Area: Duomo
Address: Via Di Porta Rossa 19 50123
Florence Italy
Phone: 055 3995913

#426
Il Granaio
Cuisines: Bistros
Average Price: Expensive
Area: Duomo
Address: Via Dei Tavolini 14R 50122
Florence Italy
Phone: 055 291027

#427
Il Bufalo Trippone
Cuisines: Tuscan, Sandwiches
Average Price: Inexpensive
Area: Duomo
Address: Via Dell'anguillara 48R 50122
Florence Italy
Phone: 055 290518

#428
O'Vesuvio
Cuisines: Pizza, Food Delivery Services
Average Price: Modest
Area: Duomo
Address: Via Dei Cimatori 21R 50122
Florence Italy
Phone: 055 285487

#429
Yummy Yummy
Cuisines: Cocktail Bars, Italian
Average Price: Modest
Area: Novoli
Address: Via Francesco Baracca 1F 50127
Florence Italy
Phone: 055 5276734

#430
Borgo Alle Fate
Cuisines: Bistros, Breweries
Average Price: Modest
Area: Duomo
Address: Borgo Degli Albizi 22R 50122
Florence Italy
Phone: 335 8088844

#431
Da Kou
Cuisines: Ramen, Sushi Bars
Average Price: Expensive
Area: Santa Maria
Address: Via Del Melarancio 21 50123
Florence Italy
Phone: 055 282922

#432
Antico Beccaria
Cuisines: Pubs, Cafes
Average Price: Modest
Area: Oberdan
Address: Piazza Cesare Beccaria 24R 50121
Florence Italy
Phone: 055 243862

#433
Hostaria Bibendum
Cuisines: Italian
Average Price: Exclusive
Area: Duomo
Address: Via Dei Pescioni 8 50123
Florence Italy
Phone: 055 2665620

#434
Nin Hao
Cuisines: Chinese
Average Price: Modest
Area: Stazione Ferroviaria Santa Maria
Address: Borgo Ognissanti 159R 50123
Florence Italy
Phone: 055 210770

#435
Trattoria Angiolino
Cuisines: Tuscan
Average Price: Expensive
Area: Palazzo Pitti
Address: Via Di Santo Spirito 36R 50125
Florence Italy
Phone: 055 2398976

#436
La Milkeria
Cuisines: Cafes, Breakfast & Brunch
Average Price: Inexpensive
Area: Duomo
Address: Borgo Degli Albizi 87R 50122
Florence Italy
Phone: 055 9756052

#437
Aviazione
Cuisines: Burgers, Pizza
Average Price: Modest
Area: Campo Di Marte
Address: Viale Malta 4 50137
Florence Italy
Phone: 055 5381058

#438
La Piazzetta
Cuisines: Pizza, Tuscan
Average Price: Modest
Area: Gavinana
Address: Piazza Del Bandino Via Di Ripoli
43R 50126 Florence Italy
Phone: 055 6800253

#439
Vico Del Carmine
Cuisines: Pizza, Seafood, Napoletana
Average Price: Modest
Area: Palazzo Pitti
Address: Via Pisana 40R 50143
Florence Italy
Phone: 055 2336862

#440
Procacci
Cuisines: Wine Bars, Sandwiches
Average Price: Modest
Area: Duomo
Address: Via Dei Tornabuoni 64R 50123
Florence Italy
Phone: 055 211656

#441
Sasso Di Dante
Cuisines: Italian
Average Price: Modest
Area: Duomo
Address: Piazza Delle Pallottole 6 50122
Florence Italy
Phone: 055 282113

#442
Mister Pizza
Cuisines: Pizza, Gluten-Free
Average Price: Inexpensive
Area: Santa Croce
Address: Via Pietrapiana 82R 50121
Florence Italy
Phone: 055 3860311

#443
Sushiko
Cuisines: Japanese,
Asian Fusion, Sushi Bars
Average Price: Modest
Area: Novoli
Address: Via Enrico Forlanini 1 50127
Florence Italy
Phone: 055 410359

#444
Masò
Cuisines: Pizza, Italian
Average Price: Expensive
Area: Santa Maria
Address: Via Maso Finiguerra 10 50123
Florence Italy
Phone: 055 212106

#445
Arà È Sud
Cuisines: Sicilian
Average Price: Expensive
Area: Duomo
Address: Via Della Vigna Vecchia 4R 50122
Florence Italy
Phone: 331 2170926

#446
Le Mossacce
Cuisines: Tuscan, Trattorie
Average Price: Expensive
Area: Duomo
Address: Via Del Proconsolo 55R 50122
Florence Italy
Phone: 055 294361

#447
L'Ortone
Cuisines: Tuscan
Average Price: Expensive
Area: Santa Croce
Address: Piazza Ghiberti 87R 50122
Florence Italy
Phone: 055 2340804

#448
Caffè Aiem
Cuisines: Italian, Cafes
Average Price: Modest
Area: Campo Di Marte
Address: Piazza Leopoldo Nobili 11 50131
Florence Italy
Phone: 055 570315

#449
Trattoria Vittoria
Cuisines: Seafood
Average Price: Expensive
Area: Palazzo Pitti
Address: Via Della Fonderia 52R 50142
Florence Italy
Phone: 055 225657

#450
La Sosta De' Golosi
Cuisines: Italian, Ice Cream, Coffee & Tea
Average Price: Modest
Area: Duomo
Address: Via Dei Pecori 8-24 50123
Florence Italy
Phone: 055 280690

#451
Caffè d'Orzo
Cuisines: Italian, Vegan, Cafeteria
Average Price: Inexpensive
Area: Fortezza Basso
Address: Via Reginaldo Giuliani 17R 50141
Florence Italy
Phone: 055 411905

#452
Pizza Man
Cuisines: Pizza
Average Price: Modest
Area: Monticelli
Address: Via Del Sansovino 191 50142
Florence Italy
Phone: 055 712738

#453
Rugbier
Cuisines: Pizza, German, Breweries
Average Price: Modest
Area: Campo Di Marte
Address: Viale Pasquale Paoli 21 50137
Florence Italy
Phone: 055 572586

#454
Gustavino
Cuisines: Wine Bars, Italian
Average Price: Expensive
Area: Duomo
Address: Via Della Condotta 37R 50122
Florence Italy
Phone: 055 2399806

#455
Gilda Bistrot
Cuisines: Italian, Bistros
Average Price: Expensive
Area: Santa Croce
Address: Piazza Ghiberti 41R 50122
Florence Italy
Phone: 055 2343885

#456
Trattoria Gargani
Cuisines: Italian
Average Price: Expensive
Area: Santa Maria
Address: Via Del Moro 48R 50123
Florence Italy
Phone: 055 2398898

#457
Osteria Delle Brache
Cuisines: Pizza, Italian
Average Price: Modest
Area: Duomo
Address: Piazza Dei Peruzzi 5R 50122
Florence Italy
Phone: 055 215420

#458
Dioniso
Cuisines: Greek
Average Price: Expensive
Area: Indipendenza
Address: Via San Gallo 16R 50129
Florence Italy
Phone: 055 217882

#459
5 E Cinque
Cuisines: Tuscan, Vegetarian
Average Price: Modest
Area: Palazzo Pitti
Address: Piazza Della Passera 1 50121
Florence Italy
Phone: 055 2741583

#460
Il Conte Ugolino
Cuisines: Pizza, Italian
Average Price: Modest
Area: Palazzo Pitti
Address: Via Senese 17 50124
Florence Italy
Phone: 055 222127

#461
l'Toscano
Cuisines: Italian, Gluten-Free, Vegan
Average Price: Expensive
Area: Santa Maria
Address: Via Guelfa 70R 50129
Florence Italy
Phone: 055 215475

#462
Le Botteghe Di Donatello
Cuisines: Italian
Average Price: Modest
Area: Duomo
Address: Piazza Duomo 28R 50122
Florence Italy
Phone: 055 216678

#463
Libreria Brac
Cuisines: Cafes, Bookstores, Vegetarian
Average Price: Modest
Area: Duomo
Address: Via Dei Vagellai 18R 50122
Florence Italy
Phone: 055 0944877

#464
The Goose Bistro
Cuisines: Bistros, Bars, British
Average Price: Modest
Area: Duomo
Address: Via Delle Oche 15R 50122
Florence Italy
Phone: 055 2654511

#465
Kome
Cuisines: Japanese
Average Price: Expensive
Area: Duomo
Address: Via Dè Benci 41R 50122
Florence Italy
Phone: 055 2008009

#466
Enotria
Cuisines: Italian, Wine Bars
Average Price: Expensive
Area: Stazione Ferroviaria Santa Maria
Address: Via Delle Porte Nuove 50 50144
Florence Italy
Phone: 055 354350

#467
A Casa Mia
Cuisines: Pizza, Barbeque
Average Price: Modest
Area: Monticelli
Address: Via Pisana 165R 50143
Florence Italy
Phone: 055 7390449

#468
Ino
Cuisines: Sandwiches
Average Price: Modest
Area: Duomo
Address: Via Georgofili 3 50122
Florence Italy
Phone: 055 219208

#469
The Diner
Cuisines: American (Traditional), Diners,
Breakfast & Brunch
Average Price: Modest
Area: Duomo
Address: Via Dell'acqua 2 50122
Florence Italy
Phone: 055 290748

#470
Chalet Bellariva
Cuisines: Pizza, Italian, Seafood
Average Price: Exclusive
Area: Campo Di Marte
Address: Lungarno Cristoforo Colombo 11
50136, Florence Italy
Phone: 055 667082

#471
L'angolo Del Gusto
Cuisines: Pizza
Average Price: Modest
Area: Fortezza Basso
Address: Via Taddeo Alderotti 37 50134
Florence Italy
Phone: 055 435718

#472
La Piperna
Cuisines: Tuscan, Pizza
Average Price: Modest
Area: Michelangelo
Address: Via Giampaolo Orsini 60 50126
Florence Italy
Phone: 055 5270661

#473
Palle D'oro
Cuisines: Trattorie, Tuscan
Average Price: Modest
Area: Santa Maria
Address: Via Sant'Antonino 43R 50123
Florence Italy
Phone: 055 288383

#474
Tre Lire
Cuisines: Italian, Lounges
Average Price: Modest
Area: Santa Maria
Address: Via Della Scala 8 50123
Florence Italy
Phone: 055 2741613

#475
Cuculia
Cuisines: Bookstores, Vegetarian, Cafeteria
Average Price: Modest
Area: Palazzo Pitti
Address: Via Dei Serragli 3R 50124
Florence Italy
Phone: 055 2776205

#476
Osteria Zio Gigi
Cuisines: Italian
Average Price: Modest
Area: Duomo
Address: Via Portinari Folco 7R 50122
Florence Italy
Phone: 055 215584

#477
Ok Bar
Cuisines: Cafes, Italian, Breakfast & Brunch
Average Price: Modest
Area: Duomo
Address: Via Dei Servi 97R 50122
Florence Italy
Phone: 055 217149

#478
Satori
Cuisines: Japanese, Lounges, Asian Fusion
Average Price: Expensive
Area: Piazza Della Liberta/Savonarola,
Campo Di Marte
Address: Via Antonio Pacinotti 5R 50131
Florence Italy
Phone: 055 571312

#479
La Cité
Cuisines: Bookstores, Venues & Event
Spaces, Cafeteria
Average Price: Modest
Area: Palazzo Pitti
Address: Borgo San Frediano 20R 50124
Florence Italy
Phone: 055 210387

#480
Red Garter
Cuisines: Pubs, Karaoke, Steakhouses
Average Price: Modest
Area: Santa Croce
Address: Via Dei Benci 33R 50125
Florence Italy
Phone: 055 2480909

#481
Cinto Cucina In Torre
Cuisines: Tuscan
Average Price: Modest
Area: Duomo
Address: Via Palmieri 35 50122
Florence Italy
Phone: 055 245430

#482
Il Barone Di Porta Romana
Cuisines: Vegan, Vegetarian
Average Price: Modest
Area: Palazzo Pitti
Address: Via Romana 123R 50125
Florence Italy
Phone: 055 2335132

#483
Sei Divino!
Cuisines: Wine Bars, Tuscan, Cocktail Bars
Average Price: Modest
Area: Santa Maria
Address: Borgo Ognissanti 42R 50123
Florence Italy
Phone: 055 215794

#484
Lima Limon
Cuisines: Peruvian
Average Price: Modest
Area: Le Cascine
Address: Via Del Ponte Alle Mosse 117A
50144, Florence Italy
Phone: 055 9333820

#485
Il Panino Tondo
Cuisines: Breakfast & Brunch, Burgers
Average Price: Modest
Area: Stazione Ferroviaria Santa Maria
Address: Via Montebello 56R 50123
Florence Italy
Phone: 055 290265

#486
Trattoria Tiberio
Cuisines: Italian
Average Price: Expensive
Area: Indipendenza
Address: Via Delle Ruote 26R 50129
Florence Italy
Phone: 055 3841266

#487
Tepidario Del Roster
Cuisines: Cafes, Bars
Average Price: Inexpensive
Area: Fortezza Basso
Address: Via Vittorio Emanuele 4 50139
Florence Italy
Phone: 055 499334

#488
Gallo Bianco
Cuisines: Chinese
Average Price: Inexpensive
Area: Oberdan
Address: Via Scialoia 4R 50100
Florence Italy
Phone: 055 2476289

#489
Biancorosso
Cuisines: Japanese, Italian
Average Price: Modest
Area: Duomo
Address: Via Maurizio Bufalini 9R 50122
Florence Italy
Phone: 055 218956

#490
Crepapelle
Cuisines: Creperies, Sandwiches, Vegan
Average Price: Modest
Area: Michelangelo
Address: Via Giampaolo Orsini 55 50126
Florence Italy
Phone: 338 5401580

#491
Wabi Sabi
Cuisines: Japanese
Average Price: Expensive
Area: Campo Di Marte
Address: Viale Dei Mille 53 50131
Florence Italy
Phone: 055 587779

#492
Koto
Cuisines: Ramen
Average Price: Modest
Area: Santa Croce
Address: Via Verdi 42R 50122
Florence Italy
Phone: 055 2479477

#493
Il Cardellino
Cuisines: Italian
Average Price: Modest
Area: Indipendenza
Address: Via San Gallo 37R 50129
Florence Italy
Phone: 055 475090

#494
Ararat Le Bracerie
Cuisines: Fast Food, Armenian
Average Price: Modest
Area: Le Cascine
Address: Via Giuseppe Galliano 150A 50144
Florence Italy
Phone: 331 3042633

#495
Yagura
Cuisines: Japanese
Average Price: Expensive
Area: Palazzo Pitti
Address: Via Pisana 16R 50143
Florence Italy
Phone: 055 223145

#496
La Divina Commedia
Cuisines: Italian
Average Price: Modest
Area: Duomo
Address: Via Dei Cimatori 7R 50122
Florence Italy
Phone: 055 215369

#497
La Tavernetta Del Battistero
Cuisines: Italian, Pizza
Average Price: Modest
Area: Duomo
Address: Via Dei Servi 52 50122
Florence Italy
Phone: 055 286109

#498
Cafaggi
Cuisines: Italian
Average Price: Expensive
Area: Indipendenza
Address: Via Guelfa 35R 50129
Florence Italy
Phone: 055 294989

#499
Boccascena
Cuisines: Italian
Average Price: Modest
Area: Gavinana
Address: Viale Europa 49 50126
Florence Italy
Phone: 055 685996

#500
Trattoria L'oriuolo
Cuisines: Tuscan, Trattorie
Average Price: Modest
Area: Duomo
Address: Via Dell'oriuolo 58R 50122
Florence Italy
Phone: 055 2260255

Made in United States
Orlando, FL
17 February 2022